# Chauvinist Or Feminist?

## Paul's View of Women

### RICHARD and JOYCE BOLDREY
### Foreword by David M. Scholer

 A CANON PRESS BOOK

**BAKER BOOK HOUSE**
Grand Rapids, Michigan

This essay originally appeared under the title "Women in Paul's Life" in *Trinity Studies* 22 (1972): 1–36, and is reprinted here by permission.

Quotations from Ronald A. Knox, trans., *The Holy Bible (Knox)* are copyrighted by Burns and Oates, 1954; from James Moffatt, trans., *A New Translation of the Bible (Moffatt)*, by Hodder and Stoughton, 1926; from the *New American Standard Bible* (NASB), by The Lockman Foundation, 1960, 1962, 1963, 1968, 1971, 1972; from *The New English Bible* (NEB), by Oxford University and Cambridge University Presses, 1961, 1970; from J. B. Phillips, trans., *The New Testament in Modern English (Phillips)*, by Macmillan, 1960; and from *The Holy Bible: Revised Standard Version* (RSV), by the Division of Christian Education of the National Council of Churches of Christ in the United States of America, 1946, 1952, 1971. Scripture quotations are from the RSV unless otherwise specified.

*To
our friend
Donna*

# Contents

# Foreword

Raymond E. Brown, undoubtedly the leading Roman Catholic Biblical scholar in the United States, has included the ordination of women as one of the five crises facing the church.[1] Even though Brown referred primarily to the Roman Catholic church, his perception of the status of women in the church as a major religious-ecclesiastical crisis is certainly correct.

In a special sense, I believe that the place of women in the church and its ministry, as well as the nature of Christian marriage, are now, and will be even more so in the future, sensitive and crucial issues for evangelical Christianity. Because *Chauvinist or Feminist? Paul's View of Women* is written and published by evangelicals and is directed specifically to an evangelical audience, it is important for the discussion of these issues.

The Boldreys' book assumes importance in part because so little evangelical literature seriously argues, with attention to Biblical detail, the case for the equality of the sexes in all spheres of life, including the church. Much evangelical writing on this subject argues for traditional principles

1. *Biblical Reflections on Crises Facing the Church* (New York: Paulist, 1975).

9

of female subordination to males and the exclusion of women from the church's ministry. Most of the evangelical literature which argues for the equality of the sexes does so either in a very popular format or within a relatively complex theological or ecclesiastical, rather than exegetical, framework. The Boldreys have recognized that within evangelical Christianity (and in many other Christian traditions, too) the argument over the place of women in the church and the nature of Christian marriage always comes back to arguments about the meaning of certain passages in the Bible. Thus, they have chosen to write about Paul's view of women (with more emphasis on marriage than ministry) since it is in the Pauline literature that the majority of the crucial texts occur. (They do give brief attention to Genesis 2–3 in the context of Paul's references to the Old Testament and one footnote to Jesus in the Gospels, the other major areas of Biblical concern; see also women in Acts and I Peter 3:1–7.)

One of the strengths of the Boldreys' book is that it takes the exegetical task seriously, examining the pertinent Pauline texts in considerable detail. All Christians who accept the practical authority of what the Biblical canon affirms should grapple with the data and the arguments that the Boldreys present. Of course not everyone will be convinced of every interpretation offered here. This will be true of readers from whatever side of the issue they come. In fact, I suspect that intensive exegetical concern with the Pauline texts—and with others on women and marriage—is, especially in evangelical circles, still in its youth. Debates over the interpretation of the many details of the crucial texts will continue. In this context I am happy to commend the Boldreys' work both for its serious, detailed exegesis of the Pauline texts (for example, note the fine comments on I Corinthians 7:3–5, a text too often neglected) and for its conclusions that the Biblical texts favor the equality of the sexes in all spheres of life, including the church and its ministry. (The concept of equality is not to be equated with absolute uniformity; it does not deny God's creation of sexual differentiation and does not necessarily determine in advance how at least some traditional sexual role expectations in a given culture may or may not be altered.)

Underlying the different interpretations of Biblical passages by serious exegetes is hermeneutics—the methodology of interpretation and of our application of its results to

Christian life today. The Boldreys' recognition of the hermeneutical issues and their refusal to accept too simplistic an assessment of such issues also make their book important.

People who attempt to face these issues squarely are often charged with avoiding "the simple recognition of what the Bible says." It is precisely the concern for "what the Bible says" that is at issue. In my experience, those who see the raising of hermeneutical issues as a "smoke screen" that obscures the "clear," "simple," "obvious" meaning of the text, that refuses to "let the Bible speak for itself," fail to recognize that what they consider to be the text's "obvious meaning" is an interpretation of the text. Because they often have adopted these interpretations from their tradition or from an authoritative source, they do not realize that these interpretations required hermeneutical decisions.

The Boldreys recognize two aspects of the hermeneutical issue that I find particularly important. One is *consistency*. Those opposed to equal status for women in marriage and the church often press such texts as I Timothy 2:12, claiming that the "clear teaching of Scripture" obviously prohibits women from exercising any authority in the church's ministry, and that if one accepts Scripture's authority, the issue is closed. It is to the Boldreys' credit that they accept the authority of Scripture and at the same time press for consistency in accounting for all of the Biblical data. Hence, Paul's comments on Phoebe in Romans 16:1ff must be accounted for in any final decision on the intention and application of I Timothy 2:12; and II Corinthians 11:3 must be considered when interpreting I Timothy 2:14. This should warn against the "absolutization" of one sentence of Scripture without regard for the consistency of the whole. Further, this care for consistency delivers the Boldreys from giving too much attention to Galatians 3:28 while giving too little to other relevant texts.

The other aspect of the hermeneutical issue that I would stress is that of *context*. The Boldreys clearly and correctly assess many aspects of the position and status of women in the cultural milieu in which Paul lived, thought, and wrote his letters. They point out that Paul's injunctions in I Corinthians 11 and 14 and in I Timothy 2, which form the basis for the traditional interpretation that women are to be subordinate and silent, reflect both Paul's culture and his genuine and practical acceptance, but not eternal endorsement, of certain of these cultural factors.

Objectors often say that whenever one allows cultural factors to limit the intent or application of a text in time, it is tantamount to denying the Bible's timeless authority. They sometimes argue that although some or all texts are culturally influenced, they are *in toto* timeless and applicable without discrimination. Any claim to isolate those cultural factors and to distinguish them from the transcultural intentions and applications of a text is seen as a covert means for substituting one's own ideas for God's truth.

It can and must be admitted that there are no simple rules for distinguishing between that which is culturally conditioned and that which is not when interpreting a Biblical text. Failure to acknowledge this is, in my judgment, failure to recognize the very character of the Scriptural revelation of God: genuine human-historical documents produced in specific social-cultural contexts. Thus, the interpreter must be sensitive to all the factors of the historical tradition and context in which a text was written. Although most serious interpreters of Scripture give theoretical assent to this, I believe too few pursue its actual implications when handling the texts dealing with the status of women.

As these observations suggest, I believe that much of the intraevangelical hermeneutical strife could be averted if much of what is termed "culturally relative" would be termed instead "historically conditioned." That God's supreme revelation, Jesus Christ, was historically conditioned is established beyond question by the fact of the incarnation. God, in His infinite wisdom, chose to reveal Himself in and through a genuine human person who lived in a specific time, place, and culture. This is also, as indicated, the case with the canonical revelation of God, including the statements of Paul.

I happily commend the Boldreys' book because it seriously and courageously proceeds with the hermeneutical sensitivity which I believe is so necessary for the progress of the discussion concerning contemporary issues relating to the status and roles of women. This "progress of the discussion" is what, quite frankly, concerns me. I sense that the issues related to the equal status of women in marriage and in the ministry threaten to bring harmful controversy and even divisiveness into the church. The

Boldreys point with patience in the right direction. It is my ardent hope that this book will move us all toward a proper and peaceful acceptance of the privilege and responsibility of every Christian, male and female, to mutual submission in Christ in marriage or in singleness and to service in any position in the ministry, as God calls His people.

It is commonly assumed, in evangelical and other conservative sectors of the church, that for an exegete to conclude that women have equal status is simply a capitulation to the women's liberation movement of the sixties and seventies. I hope that the Boldreys' book will help show that not just the "feminists," but the "traditionalists" as well, bring their cultural presuppositions about sexual identity and roles to the text, presuppositions that often distort proper historical exegesis. Thus, I hope that this book will encourage further disciplined exegetical and hermeneutical study, not only of Paul, but of the other pertinent Biblical texts as well.

DAVID M. SCHOLER
Associate Professor of New Testament
Gordon-Conwell Theological Seminary

# Preface

The four years that have elapsed since we completed this study have confirmed in our minds the validity of all its arguments and applications. Paul, a true messenger of Christ, was indeed a radical. The principle of no "male and female" in Christ must be accepted with all its ramifications.

In our day such principles of male-female interaction constitute what is called *Christian feminism*. The latter term is indicative of the tensions that exist, especially within the marriage relationship. Our study has presented some of the problems engendered by seeking to apply Christ's law of love to a culture that is governed by other norms. We have not, however, dealt enough with the conflicts that can come about in a single relationship when a husband and wife seek to apply these principles to their own marriage.

For example, what happens to the female when she decides no longer to manipulate a male out of her "weakness" or to "love him" for his "strength"? She suddenly finds herself even more powerless, more crushable, than before. And what happens to the male who no longer desires to "lord it over" a female or to "love her" for her "weakness"? He is suddenly lost in a world that measures power by intellectual superiority or force.

The main problem is not that we refuse to relinquish traditional roles. It is that we each, male and female, seek the one role not intended for us—the role that is God's alone. We wish at all costs to preserve ourselves, our pride, and our ability to operate. We choose cultural definitions to help us do that. The problem is that people sincerely give up their traditional roles without also giving up their need to be in complete control. Wives become intoxicated with the idea of freedom; husbands rebel at the destruction of their "given" rights. Chaos results.

Ironically, Sarah—the eternal example for Christian women—can also be an example for Christian men. Sarah was powerless. She trusted in God, then obeyed her husband who used her deceitfully in his weakness. When men believe that their rights have been wrested from them in the name of Christ and that they have been made fools in the eyes of their fellows, let them also, like Sarah, understand that true power belongs to neither them nor their spouses, but to the Lord. The Lord always keeps those who, like Sarah, trust Him.

This is most difficult, yet crucial. Otherwise it is too easy for a husband to agree with the world of men who cry out: "Don't give in! They just want to take over!"

But there is an answer. A man who desires to follow Christ's teaching concerning the husband's role should be gentle with himself, not expecting immediate changes of heart, not giving up when he fails. A woman, on the other hand, must realize that freedom comes in two stages. The first is to move from the security of having a "place" where she is not fully responsible for her actions to a freedom found through faith. The second is to live as a mature person without flaunting her freedom. This involves accepting her husband, wherever he is, and realizing that there is no transition more painful than the one that involves giving up power—especially in our power-oriented, male-dominated society. It is often easier to strive for freedom than to step down from power.

Today, as in Paul's time, Greeks, Jews, slaves, masters, women, and men all desire freedom from the bondage of tyranny, be it of world powers or of a culture that prescribes roles. But the only true freedom is putting Christ to the test and, in trust, accepting His yoke, the law of love.

Our sincerest thanks to Dr. David M. Scholer for his

foreword, to Dr. Donald W. Dayton for the annotated bibliography, and to *Trinity Studies* (now *Trinity Journal*) for the permission to reprint this study.

# List of
# Abbreviations

18

# Introduction 1

## Paul's Women Friends

"Paul was a rash and not very deep man, as his contempt for women shews," declared George Bernard Shaw.[1] With his reputation of reverence toward intelligent women, Shaw would have done well to check the list of church leaders that Paul included at the close of his letter to the Romans. Among the twenty-six names are those of eight women. Persis, Mary, Tryphoena ("Dainty"), Tryphosa ("Delicate"), Julia, and Junia[2] are otherwise unknown, but

---

1. The Intelligent Woman's Guide to Socialism and Capitalism (New York: Brentano, 1928), p. 3.
2. Romans 16:6, 7, 12, 15. Concerning Junia, John Chrysostom, a bishop of the early church, exclaimed: "Oh! How great is the devotion of this woman, that she should be counted worthy of the appellation of apostle." Quoted in Elsie Gibson, When the Minister Is a Woman, p. 10. However, because of grammatical ambiguity we cannot know whether the Greek name is feminine or masculine. Most contemporary commentators (male) suggest that the name is masculine because of the context (a case of a priori reasoning). Most ancient commentators understood it as feminine. Assuming the latter, there remains another problem: Does the statement that Junia and Andronicus were "of note among the apostles" mean that Junia was an apostle, or that she was well known among the apostles (cf. the use of episēmos, "notorious," in Matt. 27:16)?

there is more specific information about the responsibilities of Phoebe and Prisca.

It is generally agreed, as the KJV subscript after 16:27 indicates, that Phoebe carried Paul's brilliant theological treatise from Corinth, where it was written, to Rome (16:1f likely was her introduction to Christians there), a distance of several hundred miles. Such a journey required courage and stamina in those times and was considered a task only for officials.[3] Phoebe's qualifications included her position[4] in the church at Cenchreae, the eastern port of Corinth. She probably also served in the capacity of patroness[5] to Paul and other Christian workers.

Prisca,[6] a reputable teacher,[7] was highly regarded by her colleague Paul and by all the churches among the Gentiles. Paul and Timothy (Acts 18:5; Rom. 16:21) had met her and Aquila, her husband, in Corinth and stayed with them for a year and a half. Then the four traveled to Ephesus, where Prisca and Aquila's "house church" (I Cor. 16:19)

---

3. Ibid., p. 9.

4. See NEB on Romans 16:1. The Greek work is *diakonos*, which appears twenty-two times in the New Testament. In the KJV it is rendered "minister" eighteen times, "deacon" three times, and "servant" only in this passage! The translation "deaconess" (RSV, *Phillips*, etc.) is also misleading, for the separate office for women was established long after Phoebe died; in the early church both men and women were "deacons." The grammar of the word (*diakonos* is a two-terminal adjective) does not even distinguish between "deacon" and "deaconess."

5. The Greek word *prostatis* is translated "succourer" in the KJV. The masculine (*prostatēs, patronus* in Latin) "was the title of a citizen in Athens who took charge of the interest of *metoikoi* (clients) and persons without civic rights." James Denney, *St. Paul's Epistle to the Romans,* in EGT, 2:718.

6. Romans 16:3–5. The other relevant passages are Acts 18 and I Corinthians 16:19. It is interesting that Luke three times calls her Priscilla (with the so-called "diminutive ending" that signifies endearment or close friendship), while Paul three times uses the more formal Prisca, perhaps for the same reason that he called Persis "the beloved" rather than "my beloved" as he refers to men in vv. 8f.

7. The Greek word translated "helpers" in the KJV is *synergos,* literally "fellow worker." It is the same word used by Paul of Timothy in verse 21 and again in I Thessalonians 3:2, and of Luke in Philemon 24. As Charles C. Ryrie admitted, "It would be difficult to prove that the 'helping' did not include public teaching and even possibly missionary work." *The Place of Women in the Church,* p. 55. Acts 18:26 presents her as a cultured and educated person, a teacher of Apollos.

20

served as a base for their ministry to the Ephesians; after Paul left for Syria, Timothy headed the church. Paul eventually reached Rome (cf. II Tim. 4:19), and good grounds exist to suggest that later Prisca joined him and from there wrote the Letter to the Hebrews (who lived in Ephesus).[8]

While in Syria, Paul and Luke visited in the home of Philip, whose four daughters "prophesied" (Acts 21:9; this Old Testament word was usually appropriated in the New Testament for the office of general preaching and teaching). Elsie Gibson thought that Luke's reference to these women hints that they had assisted in his compilation of gospel events.[9] If so, Paul too would have benefited from their ministry.

Other leaders in their respective assemblies were Apphia, Philemon's wife (Philem. 2), and Euodia and Syntyche in Philippi (Phil. 4:2f). William Ramsay[10] saw one of the latter two as the "Lydia" of Acts 16 who, though she resided and carried on her business in Philippi, was a native of Thyatira, a city in Lydia. "Lydia" was one of a group of women who listened to Paul's first sermon in Philippi, and she and her household were his initial European converts. Whether or not Ramsay is correct, we know (because of the use of the participle *idontes* in Acts 16:40) that the church did congregate in her house, and it is likely, because this was a new work, that her ministry went beyond that of being hospitable; she probably was one of those to whom Paul referred as having "labored at my side" (Phil. 4:3).

## Paul's Teachings

Paul's relationships with these women notwithstanding, Elizabeth Cady Stanton, foremost American leader of the nineteenth-century woman's-rights movement,[11] anticipat-

---

8. That Priscilla wrote the "unsigned" Letter to the Hebrews was the view of Harnack, Harris, Peake, Moulton, and Schiele. A good modern defense of the theory is found in Ruth Hoppin, *Priscilla: Author of the Epistle to the Hebrews.*

9. Gibson, *When the Minister Is a Woman,* p. 11.

10. *St. Paul the Traveller and the Roman Citizen* (London: Hodder and Stoughton, 1908), p. 214.

11. Stanton (1815–1902), daughter of a judge and wife of an abolitionist, helped organize the first U.S. woman's-rights convention at Seneca Falls, New York, in 1848. For it she prepared her famous woman's bill of rights and resolutions, among which was the first

ing the uncomfortable and usually private feelings of many twentieth-century Christians, said: "Whatever the Bible [and she did not exclude the Pauline epistles] may be made to do in Hebrew or Greek, in plain English it does not exalt and dignify women."[12] Stanton and other rebellious feminists rejected outright the Biblical teachings about women as so much pabulum they were no longer willing to swallow, seldom arguing that the Bible had been misinterpreted. All of them had heard too often what Paul had to say about women:

> ... man [was not] created for woman, but woman for man (I Cor. 11:9).

> [Young women are] to be ... domestic, kind, and submissive to their husbands.... (Titus 2:5; cf. Eph. 5:22, 24, 33; Col. 3:18).

> [Young widows are] gossips and busybodies.... I would have ... [them] marry [and] bear children.... (I Tim. 5:13f).

> Let a woman learn in silence with all submissiveness. I permit no woman to teach or to have authority over men; she is to keep silent. For ... Adam was not deceived, but the woman was deceived and became a transgressor (I Tim. 2:11–14; cf. I Cor. 14:34f).

They accepted without question that woman's inferiority to man is the clear doctrine of Scripture, a conclusion endorsed today by most superficial students of the Bible.

Man, it is said, was created in the image and glory of God, but woman is only indirectly related to Him through her male companion. Though as a Christian she has equal claim to God's grace, her place is one of subjection to man. It is by submission to the male, her "head" and earthly "authority," that she demonstrates her subjection to the Lord. Man must rule over her and she must defer in silence, for somehow she, the "weaker" sex, is innately incapable of governing herself. Instead of obeying Adam, Eve, more gullible than her husband, fell for Satan's line and turned the authority-submission rule upside down. With the curse God reinstituted the rule and made it even more severe,

---

public demand for the right of American women to vote. Although for the next forty years she and Susan B. Anthony were the most respected leaders of the movement in this country, her radically negative reaction to the Bible and Christianity was shared by few feminists.

12. WB, 1:12.

so that subsequently woman's lot has been pain in childbirth and an inability to live without a man to rule over
her. A good woman knows that this is her place and thanks
the Lord for it.

Krister Stendahl valiantly suggested that Prisca, Phoebe,
and other female leaders carried out their responsibilities
within these limitations.[13] But this does not explain the ap-
parent discrepancy between I Timothy 2:12 (a woman is
not to teach or have authority over a man) and Romans
16:2 (Paul's own request for all the Roman Christians, male
and female, to be at Phoebe's disposal "in whatever she
may require of you").[14] And Prisca would never be called
submissive for correcting the doctrine of Apollos (Acts
18:26), a man whom Paul called his equal (I Cor. 3:5–9).
As Prisca's name precedes her husband's four of the six
times it is mentioned in the New Testament,[15] most scholars
agree that she was his intellectual superior. At least in
some respects these women were as independent as many
of their male contemporaries.

Our feeling is that the Bible is not a strait jacket for
women. As we hope to show, much of the traditional view
is half-truth, part pure conjecture, and the rest totally false.
We also hope to show that Paul's statements about woman's subordination were made within the cultural context

---

13. *The Bible and the Role of Women*, p. 42.

14. The RSV translation, "*help* her in whatever . . . for she has been
a helper of many," is misleading and too easily interpreted to mean
that as she had supplied financial aid to others, they were to extend
the same kind of help to her in her present predicament. That she
may have been a patroness we have acknowledged (see above, n. 5).
But the RSV fails to clarify the distinction between the two words
for "help": the first (*paristēmi*), used of the Romans, means they
were to "stand by" her, to provide any kind of support she might
need in her ministry; the second (*proistēmi*; cf. I Tim. 5:17; I Thess.
5:12), used of her, means that she had "stood forth" as a leader,
ruler, or supervisor (cf. Ryrie, *Women in the Church*, p. 87).

15. She is mentioned first in Acts 18:18, when she and Aquila, with
Paul, left Corinth; in Acts 18:26, when they taught Apollos in
Ephesus; in Romans 16:3, when Paul calls them his "fellow workers";
and in a similar greeting in II Timothy 4:19. Both times that Aquila
is named first can be accounted for by the cultural situation: in
Acts 18:2, where Luke introduces them to his readers in the habitual
terms of the day, "Aquila and his woman"; and in I Corinthians
16:19 ("Aquila and Prisca together with the church that is in their
house") where Paul mentions Aquila first because in that day the
house was considered Aquila's even though it was probably Prisca's
money that bought it.

of his day. As for Phoebe, Prisca, and the others, Paul's all-encompassing commitment to the gospel forced him to give responsibility to the most qualified person, regardless of sex.[16] On the other hand, he acknowledged as a cultural fact that the average woman of his day was inferior to her male counterpart and was, therefore, often incapable of acting without supervision.

Calvin Miller accounted for both aspects of Paul's response to women by calling him a moderate who allowed neither radical feminism nor the right-wingism of "evangelicals who have incorrectly represented Paul's views on womanhood."[17] But Miller solved the problem by blurring the issue. Paul's proclamation to the Galatians (3:28 *Phillips*) "Gone is the distinction between Jew and Greek, slave and free man, male and female" will always be a radical principle, while his specific statements in the areas of religion, economics, and sex ranged from liberal to conservative depending on his purposes and the conditions in which he found the churches. Gibson[18] stated most accurately what we will seek to substantiate and clarify:

> My own view is that Paul remained ambivalent on the question of female freedom. When women used their liberty with intelligence, he did not suggest curtailing their activity, but when they brought criticism upon the church, he remembered the prohibitions of his early training. Many passages in his writing, however, make it clear that for him

---

16. Such an attitude may have been fostered by what Luke, Paul's traveling companion, shared with him of Christ's liberating relations with women. Luke's information about Christ came from reliable witnesses, including Peter and Mary, Christ's mother. Putting ourselves back two thousand years makes Christ's actions, of which the following are just three of many examples, even more astounding. He rebuked the domestic Martha who was doing superbly what any good Jewish woman should have done, but showed favor to Mary who listened to Him and talked theology without helping her sister (Luke 10:38ff). When touched by the woman who had an issue of blood, He broke the Jewish taboo concerning "unclean" women by acknowledging her (Luke 8:43ff). He continually shocked His disciples and others by talking with the lowest women in public (Luke 7:36ff). Of the four Gospel writers Luke has included the largest number of references to Christ's relationships with women (cf. 1:24ff; 2:6f, 36ff; 7:11ff; 8:41f, 49ff; 12:53; 13:10ff; 14:26; 15:8ff; 16:18; 18:1ff; 21:1ff; 23:27ff, 54ff; 24:1ff).

17. "St. Paul and the Liberated Woman," *Christianity Today*, 6 August 1971, pp. 13f.

18. *When the Minister Is a Woman*, chap. 3, n. 3.

Christ superseded the law and abolished all privilege based on race, class, or sex.

The problem phrase is "he remembered the prohibitions of his early training," because it brings to the fore the mind set in which we approach the Bible. Gibson herself raised the question: "Is the subordination of woman to man a part of revelation, or a characteristic of the social setting in which the revelation occurs, or are the two so interwoven that the effort to separate them would destroy revelation itself?"[19] Before we can make a thorough exegesis of the relevant passages, we must decide to what extent Paul's words are God's words. Are they God's incontrovertible commands to us today? Or are they only "the unilluminated utterance of Paul, the man, biased by prejudice"?[20]

## The Hermeneutical Question

The problem is nonexistent for interpreters who, ironically, respect Paul too much to believe he could have written the passages under question. Ellen Battelle Dietrick described these passages as "bare-faced forgeries, interpolated by unscrupulous bishops, during the early period in which a combined and determined effort was made to reduce women to silent submission."[21] Scholars who are less rash suggest that Paul did not write the pastoral letters, and that I Corinthians 14:34f was added by "a later editor who, believing I Timothy 2:11–12 to have been written by Paul, incorporated it here."[22] But we cannot accept an interpretation that requires the a priori extraction of disagreeable passages. The overwhelming burden of proof is on those who resort to such evasions. Comparing II Corinthians 11:3 with I Timothy 2:14 gives the strong impression that these are the thoughts of the same man. And Albrecht Oepke's statement that I Corinthians 14:34f is "not beyond suspicion on textual grounds"[23] because some

---

19. Ibid., pp. 73f.

20. Lucinda B. Chandler, on I Timothy 2, in WB, 2:162. Others similarly speak of Paul's "Pharisaic prejudices" and "rabbinic reasoning," as if the apostle who wrote the manifesto in Galatians 3:28 occasionally slipped into old language patterns in speaking of women.

21. In WB, 2:149.

22. Gibson, *When the Minister Is a Woman*, chap. 3, n. 3.

23. TWNT, 1:787. Bousset, Weiss, Scott, Straatman, and others have conjectured that these two verses are a gloss or interpolation.

texts place them after verse 40 rather than interrupt the "natural" flow from verse 33 to verse 36, ignores the fact that the text as we have it is supported by the best early manuscripts and that no manuscript omits these verses altogether.

Among commentators who accept Pauline authorship are those who are concerned with his use of the Old Testament (which Paul quoted in I Corinthians 11:12 and I Timothy 2:13f and alluded to in several passages that we shall consider).[24] They point out that he was trained in the rabbinic habit of quoting fragments[25] and was consequently prone to proof-texting. Paul himself seemed to admit in I Corinthians 11:11f that his argument from the Old Testament could really go either way. But E. Earle Ellis sharply reminded us that "Paul's devotion to Scripture was not that of a rabbi; he did not cite the Scriptures from a sense of duty or a love of theology or tradition, but because of their witness to Christ."[26] To argue that New Testament authors distorted Old Testament meaning is to run the risk of establishing one's own interpretation as normative, whereas "the doctrine of verbal inspiration requires that we should accept any New Testament interpretation of an Old Testament text as legitimate."[27]

---

24. "The background of I Corinthians and I Timothy is . . . very Old Testament, the Jews having fixed the conventions to which pagan-Christians must adhere." Francine Dumas, *Man and Woman: Similarity and Difference,* p. 86. Compare Stendahl's view that the New Testament view of men and women is basically Jewish. *The Role of Women,* p. 25. E. Earle Ellis suggested that the "law" in I Corinthians 14:34 "concludes a very general reference to the teaching of serious Old Testament passages." *Paul's Use of the Old Testament* (Grand Rapids: Eerdmans, 1957), p. 22. Paul did not go to the Old Testament when dealing with purely Gentile churches in Thessalonica, Philippi, and Colossae.

25. Ellis, *Paul's Use of the Old Testament,* p. 46.

26. Ibid., p. 115. Paul did not use Old Testament proofs "like patches from a ragbag—anything to fit the argument: he did not need to resort to such expedients." Ibid., pp. 31f.

27. Roger Nicole, "New Testament Use of the Old Testament," in *Revelation and the Bible: Contemporary Evangelical Thought,* ed. Carl F. H. Henry (London: Tyndale, 1958), pp. 148f. Compare Ellis's statement: "The important consideration is not that Paul borrowed a Jewish interpretation, but that Christ's apostle, led by the Holy Spirit, used it as a true interpretation." *Paul's Use of the Old Testament,* p. 83. Nicole went on to caution, though, that to accept a New Testament interpretation of an Old Testament passage as correct "does not require that such an interpretation be necessarily viewed

Perhaps the most sophisticated feminist attempt to take
Paul seriously, but one that still falls short of the mark,
is Stendahl's booklet *The Bible and the Role of Women:
A Case Study in Hermeneutics.* It was written to both
defend the ordination of women and apply the method
of Biblical theology developed by the Uppsala school in
Sweden.[28] Stendahl made a valuable distinction between
two kinds of Biblical interpreters (hermeneuts)—the fundamentalist and the realist. His *fundamentalist* sees "the
whole [New Testament] as pure, unconditioned, essential
revelation . . . available in a pure and unambiguous form,"
a view that amounts to a "nostalgic attempt to play First
Century."[29] To harmonize disparate elements this interpreter merely dichotomizes the spiritual and the practical.
For example: under Christ there is no male or female, but
among men the weaker sex (female) should be subordinate.
The shortcoming of this stance is that it does not come
to grips with the real tension between radical Christian
concepts and an establishment society.

Stendahl's *realist* takes into account the gap of centuries.
To him the Bible teaches what is absolute "only in and
through what is relative."[30] For example, the realistic interpreter "can show how Jesus and Paul said some things in
a fashion which indicates that *they* considered them 'timeless truths.' . . . But he is also aware that they were so considered because in these respects Jesus and Paul shared
the exegetical and cultural presuppositions of their time."[31]
In short, Stendahl's Scripture is culturally bound. But the
negative implications of this position are qualified by his
understanding that the New Testament contains "elements,
glimpses, which point beyond and even 'against' the pre-
vailing view and practice of the New Testament church."[32]
Thus he can accept that some of Paul's views were built
on a *principle* concerning male and female without con-

as exclusive or exhaustive of the full Old Testament meaning."
P. 149.

28. Pp. iii–xiv, 1–5.

29. Ibid., pp. 14, 36.

30. Ibid., pp. 14, 16. The interpreter is then left with the very difficult task of deciding "whether a particular element is eternally
valid or due to the passing conditions of a former century." D. E. H.
Whiteley, *The Theology of St. Paul* (London: Blackwell, 1964), p. 233.

31. *The Role of Women,* p. 13.

32. Ibid., p. 34.

sidering a particular mandate to be "valid for all times."[33] Our view is that whatever Jesus and Paul considered truth is timeless and should be discerned by careful exegesis. We have found a solid exegetical foundation in Stendahl's work, but we think his concept that Paul's practical application and basic understanding of Christ's teaching were *both* relative, covers too much interpretive territory. For us, only Paul's practice is relative and is itself subject to exegesis. Specifically, Paul's application was not only culturally (rabbinically) conditioned but also based on "timeless truths" of Christian freedom, and it was in many respects countercultural.

Paul spoke of himself as an apostle (I Cor. 4:1–9; 15:1–11) and believed, as he wrote to the Corinthian church, that Christ was speaking through him (II Cor. 13:3).[34] Steeped though he was in Old Testament teaching, nevertheless he often did not, as had the prophets, say, "Thus saith the Lord"; rather he chose to argue more rationalistically and to wrestle with the ideas of his message.[35] Surely his per-

---

33. Ibid., p. 20. Morgan P. Noyes said that I Timothy 2 is "a case where an early Christian's understanding of the will of God needs to be corrected by the further light which God has caused to break forth from his holy Word." In IB, 11:407. A humorous expression of this same idea is found in Hoppin's essay "The Sovereignty of God and the Spiritual Status of Women": "What possessed a person like Paul to make such a crass statement: 'Man is created in the image and glory of God, but woman is not'? Paul gave the answer when he confessed: 'I have not yet reached perfection' (Phil. 3:12 NEB)." *Priscilla,* p. 128.

34. Compare also, specifically on the woman question, I Corinthians 11:1f (*paradosis* should not be translated "ordinances" as in the KJV because it refers to what Paul was "handing over" to them, that which in turn Paul had received from the Lord; cf. II Thess. 2:15) and I Corinthians 14:37 (which refers at least to the instruction about women, if not to all of chap. 14).

35. Charles Edward Cerling, Jr., in "A Wife's Submission in Marriage" (M.A. thesis, Trinity Evangelical Divinity School, 1967), spoke of "Paul's very tenuous argument" in I Corinthians 11. Indeed, Paul opens his argument with "I want you to understand" (v. 3 RSV; cf. vv. 17, 22), proceeds with an argument from the Old Testament (which he appears to weaken with the "nevertheless" parenthesis of vv. 11f), continues by asking the readers to "judge for yourselves" by looking at what "nature" teaches, and closes with a status quo argument for anyone who "insists on arguing" (v. 16 NEB). All of chapters 7–16 seems to be Paul's answers to practical questions asked by the Corinthians (cf. 7:1; 8:1). Even the harshest phrases of I Timothy 2:8–12 are introduced with "It is my desire" and "I do not permit" (the first phrase of I Timothy 3:1, incidentally, refers to what *follows;* cf. 1:15).

sonality was one factor that shaped his presentation, but more important was his calling to make known the incarnate Word, Christ, God's supreme revelation to "man" (II Cor. 1:19). His application derived from his "authority, which the Lord gave for building you up and not for destroying you" (II Cor. 10:8; 13:10). Even when it seemed Paul was not living up to this commission, he said "we cannot do anything against the truth, but only for the truth" (II Cor. 13:8).

Accordingly we will proceed with an in-depth exegesis of Paul's teaching, trying to discover the "timeless truths" that undergird his views concerning women in the churches. The inference is that our views on the woman question should coincide with Paul's, that our application, despite our different cultural setting, should still flow from the same principles. Thus, our interpretation will take all Scripture in absolute seriousness, but without involving us in the "charade of New Testament Church."

# The Old Order 2

In the light of our hermeneutic we will examine the major texts bearing on Paul's understanding of women. The two often conflicting opinions on the origin of women's subordination are (1) that it was intended by God at the beginning as part of the natural order of things and (2) that it was imposed by God after the fall, destroying paradisiacal unity between the sexes. Erik Sjoberg unequivocally presented the "order of creation" argument in his comment on I Corinthians 11:

> Paul is trying to find the most forcible argument available in order to show that his view is based on the order of nature and of creation. The order of representation expressed in the model God-Christ-man-woman and the consequences which follow therefrom have absolute validity according to Paul. To break with that is to break with God's order and with that of nature. For Paul this is not a pragmatic question but a question of principle, and a matter of deep religious conviction.[1]

1. *Exegeterna om Kvinnliga Praster* (Stockholm: SKDB, 1953), pp. 65f. Quoted in Krister Stendahl, *The Bible and the Role of Women,* p. 8. The title of Sjoberg's book means "Exegesis Concerning Women Ministers." Else Kahler was not as happy with it but was equally

Krister Stendahl summarized the "order of transgression" theory when he stated that I Timothy

> gives an unusually concrete and intelligible, essential reason for the subordination of woman.... and the decisive scriptural passage for the whole New Testament's instruction concerning the subordination of woman (Gen. 3:16) is here connected with the story of the Fall in its entirety, with the fall of Eve and the pain in childbearing which is woman's lot and therefore the "vocation" through which she will win salvation.[2]

Actually, both the arguments on woman's "total subjection" *(en pasēi hypotagēi,* 2:11) can be drawn from I Timothy ("My reasons are that man was created before woman. Further, it was Eve and not Adam who was first deceived and fell into sin," 2:13f *Phillips).* The commentary by C. F. Keil and Franz Delitzsch combines them by saying that in creation woman was "divinely appointed" to be subordinate and that the "curse" (Gen. 3:16) increased her subjection by punishing her "with a *desire* bordering upon disease."[3] J. J. Van Oosterzee made them practically indistinguishable by reasoning that the order of creation explains "why no authority was given to woman over man" and that the order of transgression tells "why she is justly forbidden to teach."[4] However, whether one makes the two orders irreconcilable or combines them, both must be examined in reference to a third, "new order" (cf. II Cor. 5:17) in Christ. Paul described it in Galatians 3:28, which we would translate as follows:

convinced that in the Pastorals "the order of creation is a stale and fixed 'order of being' which downgrades women." *Die Frau in den Paulinischen Briefen* (Zurich: Gotthelf, 1960), pp. 198–202. Quoted in Stendahl, *The Role of Women,* p. 29, n. 29. According to D. E. H. Whiteley: "It would appear that, according to even the least antifeminist interpretation of I Corinthians which is at all plausible, St. Paul did believe that women were inferior because of their sex,... [that] the sex distinction ... was still important as part of the 'natural order.' " *The Theology of St. Paul* (London: Blackwell, 1964), p. 225.

2. *The Role of Women,* p. 29. Elizabeth Cady Stanton was a rebel from Christianity for this very reason: "The real difficulty in woman's case is that the whole foundation of the Christian religion rests on her temptation and man's fall." WB, 2:214.

3. BCOT, 1:103. The argument that the "curse" is descriptive rather than prescriptive makes little difference in the long run and, at any rate, is difficult to prove.

4. *The Two Epistles of Paul to Timothy,* in CHS, 11:34.

> There is neither Jew nor Greek,
> There is neither slave nor free,
> There is no "male and female"—
> For all of you are one
> In Christ Jesus.

The main emphasis of this manifesto is Christian freedom from sin and the law, but there is also a strong allusion in the third clause to creation itself. Following the suggestion of Stendahl,[5] we put "male and female" in quotation marks. Most English translations fail to show the interruption caused by *arsen kai thēly* ("male and female") and thus miss its importance in the text. The series "neither ... nor" has been interrupted by the use of *and* because Paul quoted the words *male* and *female* (more technical than the usual *man* and *woman*) directly from Genesis 1:27— "male and female created he them" (KJV; cf. Mark 10:6 and Matt. 19:4). Paul was saying that, in Christ, relationships between men and women should transcend the male-female division.

## Creation

Before we can understand the significance of this startling idea, we must examine in detail the order of creation itself. Our principal source is I Corinthians 11:3–12 (cf. I Tim. 2:11–13). Our interpretation rests on an understanding of four key words—*head (kephalē), image (eikōn), glory (doxa),* and *power (exousia)*. We propose to demonstrate how these words support, not the traditional view that woman's status is inferior to man's, but rather that, though the historical conditions surrounding their creation differ, woman and man stand on the same plane before God.

We begin with I Corinthians 11:3–5:

> I want you to understand that the *head* of every man is Christ, the *head* of a woman is her husband, and the *head* of Christ is God. Any man who prays or prophesies with his *head* covered dishonors his *head*, but any woman who prays or prophesies with her *head* unveiled dishonors her *head*.

Paul was punning on the word *head*. When he said she "dishonors her head," he may have been referring either to her physical head or to her husband, as he did in verse 3—"the head of a woman is her husband"—which is us-

---

5. *The Role of Women*, p. 32.

ually taken to mean that woman was made to be ruled by man. A connection between headship and subordination is also suggested by the extension of the Adam/Christ parallel to include Eve and the church (cf. II Cor. 11:2). Stendahl wrote that "the order of creation for subordination is inextricably interwoven with the relation between Christ, the bridegroom, and the church as the bride."[6] The concept "Christ is the head of the church" (Eph. 5:23) is expanded elsewhere in the Letter to the Ephesians to mean that "all things are under His feet" (1:22; cf. Col. 2:10) and that He is the source of the body's smooth operation and growth (4:15f). It is also true that a strong comparison is set up between the headships of Christ and of the husband, except that the husband is not to be considered "savior of the body" (5:23 KJV; this is the reason for the "nevertheless," alla, that immediately follows in verse 24).

According to Charles C. Ryrie[7] the main point of I Corinthians 11 is that the order of heads shows that Adam could in no way be subordinate to Eve. We must also note that neither is the emphasis of the account on Eve's subordination to Adam. Rather, it seems to focus on the historical derivation of woman from man. Rosh, the Hebrew word for head, is often translated in the Septuagint by archē, the Greek word that may mean "rule" but just as often means "beginning." In this context Paul speaks of Christ, "the head of the body, the church: who is the beginning, the firstborn from the dead; that in all things he might have the preeminence" (Col. 1:18 KJV). Being the "head" is related to being "first" (but priority of time neither necessarily nor irreversibly leads to priority in rank, as we will see later, in our study of Ephesians 5). When Paul spoke of woman's head being the man, he was emphasizing man's temporal priority and woman's derivation from him; this is further substantiated by verse 8 ("woman was made from man").[8]

---

6. Ibid., p. 30.

7. The Place of Women in the Church, p. 79.

8. Lillie Devereux Blake quite missed the point when she ingeniously asserted: "It cannot be maintained that woman was inferior to man even if, as asserted in chapter II [of Genesis], she was created after him, without at once admitting that man is inferior to the creeping things, being created after them." In WB, 1:19. No comparison should be attempted here, for Paul is concerned more with "derivation" (ek, v. 8) than with temporal order per se.

Verse 9 ("woman [was created] *for* man"), though it is usually understood to mean that she was made to serve him, probably is an allusion to Genesis 2:18, "I will make him a helper fit for him." Francine Dumas[9] noted that *ezer* ("help, succor"), the word used for Eve in Genesis 2:18, is often used of God, the "helper" of His people (Exod. 18:4; Deut. 33:7; Ps. 27:9; 33:20; 94:17; 115:9–11; cf. the use of *boēthos,* the Greek cognate, in Heb. 13:6). It indicates one who comes to another's aid, who provides relief for a complaint or a need, and occurs in the Bible sixteen times of a superior, five times of an equal, but never of an inferior. Adam needed someone like him. Eve, derived from his very being, supplied that need as his equal, as himself. This is a picture of oneness, not of subordination.

We conclude that Adam is the head of Eve in the sense that (1) he was created before her and (2) she was derived from him. But in Christ male and female are interdependent (I Cor. 11:11–12, probably an incidental reference to the more explicit Gal. 3:28, the latter written first). As we shall see later, priority and position were in Paul's mind subordinate to mutuality and reciprocity.

The next proposition in the order of creation is found in I Corinthians 11:7: "For a man ought not to cover his head, since he is the *image* and *glory* of God; but woman is the *glory* of man." Here Paul built another God-man-woman chain, now in respect to "glory." He, like other rabbis, chose in this reference to Genesis 1:27 to ignore that Eve as well as Adam was created in the "image of God." Margaret E. Thrall would interpret Eve's absence to mean that Paul did not "think of the woman as existing in her own right in the Image of God."[10] But Paul's silence can hardly be proof that he did not accept what the Old Testament plainly taught. He simply limited himself to discussing the sexes in terms of *doxa* alone.

Neither does I Corinthians 11:7 imply that woman was created in man's image; it is Adam's *son* who was "after his image" (Gen. 5:1–3). All his posterity, including postdiluvian "man," is also said to be in "the image of God" (Gen. 9:6). It would seem, then, that the *imago Dei* is a definition of humanity, an inalienable quality. Whether it refers to a fundamental affinity to God, a capacity for

9. *Man and Woman: Similarity and Difference,* p. 37.

10. *The Ordination of Women to the Priesthood,* p. 67. She argued for women's ordination, but on very unorthodox "Biblical grounds."

goodness, or an innate dependence on God's will, it cannot be said to belong only to males; Eve as much as Adam was a "visible expression of the invisible God" (Col. 1:15 *Phillips*).[11]

There being no difference in the quality of their humanness, we return to Paul's contrast between male and female glory *(doxa)* and his apparently illogical conclusion. Morna D. Hooker presented the thesis in syllogistic form:

> Man is the glory of God.
> Therefore his head must be bare.
> Woman is the glory of man.
> Therefore her head must be covered.[12]

To discover what glory means for a woman and for a man, let us again look at a Hebrew word—*kabhodh* ("glory"). The word is often used in parallel with *nephesh* ("soul, self"), as in Psalm 7:5 (KJV), and therefore usually relates in some way to self-manifestation, as does "image." To state that a person is the glory of someone else is to define that person in terms of the one he reveals.[13] Ezekiel spoke of "the appearance of the likeness of the glory of Jehovah" (1:26–28 ASV). To Moses, Jehovah revealed His "glory," but only His backside, for no man has seen God and lived (Exod. 33:18ff). Christ revealed God in the flesh (John 1:14–18), and "we beheld His glory, glory as of the unique son of the Father" (v. 14 *our translation;* cf. Isa. 40:5). Christ is the "glory of God," that is, He is essentially God, a reflection of God's glory.

Man as the "glory of God" reflects the Godhead even as Christ, the second Adam, reflected God in the flesh. In the same sense woman, "the glory of man" (male), is a reflection of humanity *(adam)* itself. Looking back to creation we remember that Adam was lonely; he could not find

11. This is a reference to Christ (cf. II Cor. 4:4; Heb. 1:3), but "image" is also used in the New Testament of the "new creation" in Christ. Colossians 3:10 ("...you...have put on the new nature, which is being renewed in knowledge after the image of its creator" RSV), by referring back to Genesis 1:26, draws an analogy between "potential goodness" and "divine perfection."

12. "Authority on Her Head: An Examination of I Cor. 11:10," p. 414. Her analysis of vv. 4–7 and her thoughts on "image" and "glory" influenced our own.

13. "The 'glory of God' is, in effect, the term used to express that which men can apprehend, originally by sight, of the presence of God on earth," wrote Alan Richardson. *A Theological Word Book of the Bible* (London: SCM, 1950), p. 175.

any likeness of himself among the animals. So God formed for him Eve, from Adam's own flesh. God called him *ish* and her, *ish-ah,* a reflection of *ish.* Adam's reaction was, "I see me!" (Gen. 2:23). And Paul, when he wrote about "head" and "glory," was expressing in his way what is inherent in Adam's exclamation—that man is the source of the creation of woman.

The assumption that an unveiled head symbolized the reflection of glory can help us resolve the question of bare and covered heads. Even as Moses' face was uncovered during intercourse with God (Exod. 34:29ff; cf. II Cor. 3) and covered in the presence of the Israelites who could not stand such brilliant reflection of God's glory (II Cor. 3:13), so Paul commanded men to pray without covering their heads and thereby hiding God's glory during worship. Woman's unveiled head, however, would symbolize pride in her reflection of their humanity, which would be shameful and pretentious in the presence of God.

This understanding of Paul's desire for women to wear a head covering during worship is further substantiated by the phrase "because of the angels" (I Cor. 11:10).[14] The Scriptures often portray angels in worship situations as evidence of God's presence (cf. Ps. 137 [138]:1 in the LXX; Rev. 8:3). According to a midrash on Exodus 3:2, "Wherever Michael appears, is the Shekinah glory" (the "dwelling" of God's presence).[15] Although they should not be worshiped as God, angels can never be abstracted from God's presence. During worship a woman was not to exhibit (by uncovering her head) human glory (pride); she was to reflect God's glory. Paul's use of "because of the angels" was a more forceful way of making that point.

Paul's offering the angels as a reason for women to wear veils may explain the strong words of I Corinthians 11:6.[16]

---

14. The *dia touto* which opens the verse concludes the theological argument of vv. 3–9; therefore *dia tou angelous* appears as an unexpected afterthought. But there is too much textual evidence against its being either a gloss or the wrong words.

15. *Shemot Rabba,* 2. Quoted in TWNT, 1:81.

16. J. A. Fitzmyer, "A Feature of Qumran Angelology and the Angels of I Cor. 11:10," *New Testament Studies* 4 (1957): 48–58. This convincing article offers evidence that a "shorn head" might be considered a "bodily defect" (cf. the limitations in Lev. 21:17 23) that would offend the angels. When Fitzmyer spoke of Paul's sociological argument from "natural decency" (cf. Isa. 3:24), it is similar to our understanding of *physis* (I Cor. 11:14; cf. Rom. 2) as

We endorse the more logical possibility that, in accordance with his practice, Paul was talking simultaneously on two levels—the physical and the symbolic. Taking the second, we see in his use of the word *exousia* the core of verse 10, "For this cause ought the woman to have *power* on her head because of the angels" (KJV).

There are three major interpretations of *exousia*[17] in this verse (besides the impossible suggestion that the word refers to "magical power" contained in the veil for the purpose of warding off angels). The most common, which is seldom questioned by the average reader, makes *exousia* a symbol of the power to which a woman is subjected. Such was the function of the veil, according to the Halacha, in the practice of contemporary Judaism.[18] A Mishnah tractate on "Betrothal" states of the wife, "The power of the husband is on her."[19] And Luke 7:8, along with similar verses, seems to support this view.

However, this immediately raises the question of single women who were never required to wear veils. And we have already established that Paul's emphasis was on God's, not a man's, presence and power. But even more questionable is the consequent grammatical distortion of *exousia,* making it mean not power on her head but powerlessness. Nowhere else in Scripture can we take *exousia* in this unusual passive sense. *Echein exousian* ("to have power") always refers to one's "power to be able to do something" (cf. Matt. 7:29; 9:6; Mark 3:15; Luke 12:5; 19:17; John 10:18; 19:10; Acts 9:14; Rom. 9:21; I Cor. 7:37; Rev. 11:6; 14:18; 16:9; 18:1; 20:6), power which in the case of apocalyptic animals is located in various parts of the body (Rev. 9:3, 10, 19). In I Corinthians 9 (vv. 4, 5, 6, 12, 18) Paul used the phrase in reference to *rights* (cf. II Thess. 3:9; Heb. 13:10), and in this context we should not forget that he sanctioned the Christian woman's *exousia* over her husband's body (I Cor. 7:4). Just as today we naturally understand a crown to symbolize one's own authority, not his or her subjection to another authority, we must accept an active use of *exousia,* unless we are willing

---

"contemporary custom" (as we argued in a separate, unpublished article, "What's Natural About Hair?").

17. Fitzmyer, "The Angels of I Cor. 11:10." We follow his outline in most of the discussion which follows.

18. TWNT, 5:563.

19. Ibid., 1:361.

to accuse Paul of philological pilfering to suit his own prejudice.

An NEB marginal translation, ". . . a woman should keep *dignity* on her head for fear of the angels," is representative of the second interpretation. On the basis of I Corinthians 7:37 (where *exousia* means "control") William Ramsay and others see in 11:10 a reference to a woman's own honor and dignity. Archibald Robertson and Alfred Plummer add that for her to unveil her head would be to lose dignity and thereby give herself over to the control of others. There are stronger philological grounds to support this view than there are for the first, but contextually it stretches one's credulity.

The relatively recent (1920) interpretation forwarded by Gerhard Kittel, that *exousia* refers to authority women possess, seems most plausible. Examining the sources, we find that where a majority of New Testament manuscripts read *exousian,* some of the ancient texts read *kalumma* ("veil"). The latter could easily be accounted for as a scribe's desire to maintain consonance within the larger context. But Kittel noted that the root of the Aramaic word *sltwnyh* ("veil, ornament of the head") is the common verb *slt* ("to have power/dominion over"), the equivalent of the Greek *exousia.* We opt that Paul used the combined meaning and may have left the word in Aramaic, as is suggested by Tertullian's citations of verse 10, one time translating the word, "power," another time, "veil." And Origen, ever ambiguous, reads *kalumma kai exousian.* The argument that Paul would not have left the word in Aramaic because this would not have been understood ignores the presence of the large Jewish population in the Corinthian church (Acts 18:1–8), who would have comprehended the double meaning. Applying Kittel's interpretation of the word to woman's head, *exousia* symbolizes her power to be a daughter of God (cf. John 1:12). So the *veil* "which symbolizes the effacement of man's [humanity's] glory in the presence of God" at the same time "serves as the sign of the *exousia* which is given to the woman."[20]

In conclusion, Paul used the physical symbols "head" and "veil" to convey two spiritual realities. The first is that human beings are created not in their own image but in God's, and therefore they should show His glory, not their own, when they worship. The second is that in Christ

---

20. Hooker, "Authority on Her Head," pp. 415f.

males are not superior to females; they both "have power on their heads" to worship God. For "we all, with unveiled face, reflecting the glory of the Lord, are being changed into His image from glory to glory.... For ... God ... has shone in our hearts to give the light of the knowledge of the glory of God in the face of Christ" (II Cor. 3:18; 4:6 *our translation*).

Woman's equality before God in worship and creation apparently does not exempt her from the formidable responsibility for "man's" fall. Of her, Tertullian expostulated:

> And do you not know that you are each an Eve? The sentence of God on this sex of yours lives in this age: the guilt must of necessity live too. You are the devil's gateway: you are the unsealer of that tree: you are the first deserter of the divine law: you are she who persuaded him whom the devil was not valiant enough to attack: you destroyed so easily God's image, man. On account of your desert—that is, death, even the Son of God had to die.[21]

Bearing in mind the fragility of Tertullian's sex, let us examine the passages that served as a basis for Paul's reasoning that women should not use their power (authority) in relation to men.

## Transgression

The main New Testament reference is I Timothy 2:14 ("... and it was not Adam who was deceived; it was the woman who, yielding to deception, fell into sin," NEB), a doctrine that Lucinda B. Chandler claimed "has become a poisonous stream in Church and State."[22] Two other pertinent passages are I Corinthians 14:34 ("... the women ... should be subordinate, as even the law says"; "the law" probably refers to Genesis 3:16, though it may be more general than that) and II Corinthians 11:3 ("I am afraid that your minds may be seduced from a singlehearted devotion to him [Christ] by the same subtle means that the serpent used toward Eve," *Phillips*).

Often associated with "subordination" is a verse we have already examined, I Corinthians 11:10, "... because of the angels." Tertullian first suggested that these are "fallen angels." Since then others have taken them to be

---

21. *De Cultu Feminarum.* Quoted in Ryrie, *Women in the Church*, p. 116.

22. In WB, 2:162ff.

"seducers" and have linked their attraction to women with events of the fall itself. Pulling together unrelated New Testament references (I Cor. 7:5; II Cor. 11:3) and taking too seriously some post-first-century Jewish legends,[23] which are themselves based on apocryphal interpretations of Genesis 6:1–4,[24] Martin Dibelius and others suggest that I Corinthians 11:10 refers to a sort of magical veil necessary to ward off seductions of evil angels.[25] Recalling our more credible theory on Paul's reference to angels (pp. 37f), we also note that nowhere else does Paul use *hoi angeloi* negatively.[26] Nor is there any extra-Biblical evidence that the veil ever had such a function. We can safely state that Paul was not imputing sexual temptation to Eve.[27] In fact, the sense in which Paul feared that women might be "seduced" (II Cor. 11:3) he made clear in the following verse—they were too willing to listen to strange teachings.

Another popular assumption, whether in conjunction with or apart from the evil-angel theory, is that Eve was beguiled because of her intrinsic frailty or general womanly weakness. But there is no evidence for the assumption that

---

23. E. Earle Ellis wrote: "In Jewish writings there are several instances in which lust for Eve is viewed as Satan's motive in tempting man." Two examples are: "When the serpent copulated with Eve, he infused her with lust" and "[The Serpent] said, I will kill Adam and marry Eve." *Paul's Use of the Old Testament* (Grand Rapids: Eerdmans, 1957), p. 61.

24. See The Testament of Reuben, 5, and its relationship to II Peter 2:10f and Jude 7. Some propose that when Paul wrote I Corinthians 11:10, he was thinking, "As in the days of Noah, . . . so in the days of the Son of Man."

25. Fitzmyer, "The Angels of I Cor. 11:10," p. 52. A more popular variant on the same theme is that the veil is a means to keep the "naturally charming" women from tempting the angels—and, some would add, religious men.

26. Ibid., pp. 53ff. Fitzmyer also argued against the views that (1) Paul is using "angels" figuratively or (2) Paul means "because the angels do so" (citing Isa. 6:2). The first theory conflicts with the fact that in all of Paul's other references *hoi angeloi* means real angels. The second distorts the meaning of *dia* (the Greek preposition which, when used with the accusative case, normally refers to the cause-and-effect). The "angels" of I Corinthians 11:10 are undoubtedly "good angels."

27. See Werner Foerster's discussion in TWNT, 5:582. It is even possible that Paul used *exapataō* in II Corinthians 11:3, instead of the simpler *apataō* in Genesis 3:13, to get away from a literal rabbinic "seduction" theory.

the woman was inherently weaker than the man.[28] A second and related moot question tickled the fancy of medieval scholastics and drew tomes from their quills: "Who sinned most, Adam or Eve?" Ingenious arguments were offered on both sides, with Eve generally emerging somewhat worse than Adam. But in fact their sin was one—they both disobeyed and they both ate.[29] Paul accused them both of "transgression" (*parabasis*, of Eve in I Tim. 2:14, of Adam in Rom. 5:14; only the "order" is discussed in I Tim.), and both were cursed. Neither was more responsible; they each sinned differently. "Adam" was "one flesh"—"male and female"—in creation (Gen. 1:27f; 2:23f) and in transgression (Rom. 5:12).

The difference in their sin is that Adam's was "a simple *parabasis* (transgression)"; Eve's was "*apatē* (deception) and *parabasis* together."[30] In I Timothy 2 Paul was not primarily concerned with the *parabasis*. His attention was drawn to Eve's deception by the serpent. Adam, on the other hand, "was not deceived" either by Eve or by the serpent. It is another moot question whether he heard the serpent's argument and did not believe it, or whether he was approached by the serpent. But the question of *why* Adam sinned is important because it leads us to a reconstruction of Eve's transformation and a vital understanding of the verb *authentein* (I Tim. 2:12).

Eve, in her response to Satan, "changed the truth of God into a lie," to borrow Paul's words in Romans 1:25 (KJV). God gave her over to sin (Rom. 1:26, 28), to the capacity to become "insolent, haughty, boastful, . . . heartless, [and] ruthless" (Rom. 1:29ff). One can almost imagine her chiding tone as she said, "Hey, Adam, now I know what life is really about! Come on, you taste it, too!" as she waved the apple (or fig, as the case may be) under his nose. That Adam "hearkened" to her voice (Gen. 3:17) indicates time elapsed between her sin and his, which in turn suggests a difference in their attitudes. Paul's use of *authentein* in I Timothy 2:12 seems to suggest that Eve took advantage of the power derived from her new knowledge in order to persuade Adam to eat.

---

28. It is embarrassing to many that modern studies repeatedly show that men are more easily "sold a bill of goods" than are women.

29. John Peter Lange believed that *immah* ("with her") in Genesis 3:6 simply means that they ate together. *Genesis*, in CHS, 1:230.

30. Oosterzee, *Timothy*, loc. cit. Compare II Cor. 11:3.

*Authentein* occurs only here in the whole New Testament and has been variously translated "interrupt" (Dibelius), "have authority over" (KJV), "dictate to" *(Moffatt)*, and "domineer over" (NEB). The last two are probably closest to its essential meaning. The related noun, *authentēs,* is a loan word in rabbinics and the source of the Turkish *effendi* ("master"). *Authentein* was a popular term used to indicate an autocratic personality, one who took things into his or her own hands. For Eve to have "dictated to" Adam was to substitute a human authority for the divine. She erred not in "usurping" Adam's authority (remember Tertullian), but in usurping God's, the only authority known in the Garden before she listened to Satan.

By transgressing, woman and man shattered both their oneness with God and their oneness with each other.

# The New Order      3

The first explicit statement of Eve's submission to Adam is in the curse. Paul wrote that women "should be subordinate, as even the law [Gen. 3:16] says" (I Cor. 14:34). God never declared the curse to be good, though it may have been a fitting reversal for Eve, who had "domineered over" Adam. Now the unity between them, broken by sin, was replaced by hostility. Enmity was reinforced by the law (Eph. 2:14ff; Gal. 3:19ff) and codified into role definitions. Law (nomos) by definition indicates role (nomos is from the Greek verb nemō, "to allot," and therefore signifies "what is proper, what is assigned to someone"), and in our understanding it served as a natural starting point for assignments, imposing a necessary order on a sinful society.[1]

The resulting limitations of individual freedoms, besides making us conscious of our state of sin, also served as a "custodian" or "tutor" (paidagōgos, Gal. 3:24f; cf. II Tim.

---

1. Compare Christ's leaving His state of "equality" with God in order to enter a state of "obedience" (Phil. 2).

3:15). Insufficient in itself to promote healthy relationships,[2] the law with its consignments was a preparation for the One who came to heal our brokenness. In fact "the law with its rules and regulations" (Eph. 2:15 NEB) is the "dividing wall of hostility" (v. 14) that was abolished by our unity with Christ. Again we have returned to Galatians 3:28.

Free Jewish males daily thanked God they were not "a Gentile, a slave, or a woman."[3] But Paul asserted that these categories, with their antithetical privileges and priorities characteristic of fallen humanity and maintained by the law (cf. Exod. 20:17; Num. 27:8), were abrogated in Christ. The new order is symbolized by Christian baptism by which Gentile as well as Jew, slave as well as free, female as well as male could declare their freedom and equality. For men and women, this implies that the war between the sexes is over.

The churches, however, by and large have applied Galatians 3:28 only to "spiritual" freedom and thereby have denied women substantial social and economic opportunities. As institutions they have been too frightened to seek ways and means to apply Christ's freedom and so have stepped back and justified themselves by the older and, it would seem, safer way of the law. But Paul already had met this situation. His answer to the Galatians was, "For freedom Christ has set us free; stand fast therefore, and do not submit again to a yoke of slavery" (5:1).

Although relations between Jew and Greek were Paul's gut issue, he was also concerned with masters and slaves and with males and females. We will proceed by examining his application of the relationships.

## Jew and Greek

Speaking historically, the "Jew" preceded the Greek (Rom. 1:16); only through the Jew did the Greek come to know God. Christ limited His ministry to the "lost sheep of the house of Israel" (Matt. 15:24), spoke sharply to the Syrophoenician woman about her "place" (Mark 7:25ff), and chose only Jewish males to be His twelve apostles.

---

2. A practical way of saying, "The law cannot save." The root of the Greek word for salvation (*sōtēria*) refers to wholeness or health in every area of life.

3. William Barclay, *Letters to the Galatians and Ephesians* (Philadelphia: Westminster, 1958), p. 199.

Paul, apostle to the Gentiles (Rom. 1:5; Gal. 1:16; 2:8), accepted the historical fact but found it difficult to counter the Jew-first/Gentile-second mentality that pervaded the early Jewish church. But the Holy Spirit constrained him to assert that Jew and Greek were "fellow citizens in God's community" (Eph. 2:11f) and that circumcision, the symbol of Jewish identity, was to be abolished (cf. Acts 15; I Cor. 7:18f).

Social distinctions between Jew and Greek tested his mettle. He argued that long hair for men (orthodox Jews traditionally grew sideburns that extended to their neck and shoulders) was against "nature" (I Cor. 11:14). He reprimanded Peter who, out of fear of Jews of the circumcision party, stopped eating with Greeks and thereby limited the latter's equality in Christ to spiritual matters alone (Gal. 2). In fact that situation was the springboard for Paul's discussion of "unity in Christ" that culminated in Galatians 3:28.

From a Jew's point of view the Greek lived in a different world. The Jew's spiritual heritage influenced the totality of his attitudes.[4] But Christianity affected "the whole cultural system," including even its moral code.[5] Galatians 3:28 does not say "God loves each of you, but stay in your places"; it says that there are no longer places, no longer categories, no longer differences in rights and privileges, codes and values.

## Master and Slave

The church fathers traced the institution of slavery to the Old Testament law: "Cursed be Canaan; a slave of slaves shall he be to his brothers" (Gen. 9:25). By the first century the system of slavery "hardly recognized the hu-

---

4. A popular contemporary example is Tevye, of the Broadway musical *Fiddler on the Roof*. He had three daughters who each married against "the way it is done." After many conferences with God, Tevye acknowledged the "pledge" his first daughter had made to her boy friend and granted them his permission and blessing. The second dared not ask his permission but finally secured his blessing before leaving town to join her fiance. But the third, his favorite, married a Gentile in an Orthodox church. Tevye agonized with God but finally disowned her. He said, "No, that far I cannot go; if I bend that far I will break." His was not simply a "spiritual" decision; it involved the entire fabric of his life wrapped up in the great Jewish word *tradition*.

5. Kenneth Pike, *With Heart and Mind: A Personal Synthesis of Scholarship and Devotion* (Grand Rapids: Eerdmans, 1964), pp. 42ff.

manity of the enslaved."[6] But when Paul sent the runaway Onesimus back to Philemon,[7] he asserted that the master-slave relationship was to be circumscribed by a relationship between brothers. He asked Philemon to accept his former slave as "more than [*hyper,* 'above'] a slave, as a beloved brother, . . . both in the flesh and in the Lord" (Philem. 16). Although Paul was less adamant about social and political applications of this new attitude, by his example he implied that slavery would be ameliorated on every level such that "if it left the name of a slave, it would leave nothing but the name, and would destroy utterly the spirit and reality of the relation."[8] He set in motion a Christianizing process[9] that culminated in the early-nineteenth-century abolition of slavery in England, brought about primarily by the efforts of one Christian member of Parliament—William Wilberforce.

Paul knew that the law was too powerful a force for the subjugated ones—the Gentile, the slave, and the female—to rise above, so he asked the powerful ones to step down in love from their privileged positions. The Jewish Christians were no longer to consider the Greeks second-class Christians; masters were to offer justice and equality to their slaves (because they themselves had "a Master in heaven," Col. 4:1); and husbands were told to treat their wives as Christ related to the church (Eph. 5). Of the three applications of Christian freedom, the last is the most radical because male dominance and female subjection, one way or another, affects everyone.

## Male and Female

Ephesians 5:22–33 is the basis for our discussion of male-female relationships within the new order. We propose to show that this passage is an exciting discussion of

6. John Peter Lange, *The Epistle of Paul to Philemon,* in CHS, 11:7.

7. Philemon was a church leader in Colossae and probably a comparatively good and gentle master. Onesimus, also a Colossian (Col. 4:9), probably fled to avoid deserved punishment. Paul sent him back with the request that Philemon receive Onesimus "no longer as a slave" (v. 16). Philemon probably did set Onesimus free (see v. 21), and tradition (*Canon. Apost.* 73 and *Constit. Apost.* 7:46) says that Paul ordained the former slave as bishop of the Beroean church in Macedonia and that he was later martyred at Rome.

8. Lange, *Philemon,* in CHS, 11:20.

9. See Philip Schaff, *History of the Christian Church,* 8 vols. (Grand Rapids: Eerdmans, 1910), 2:348–51; 3:115–21.

the interdependence of two free people in Christ. That feminists consider it to be one of the major slurs against women in the New Testament is warranted by such chauvinism as is present in the commentary of Charles Hodge, a highly respected theologian of the nineteenth century. In 1856 he wrote, "It is a fair inference from our passage, that for a wife to vote independently would be a disturbance of the relation as ordained by God."[10] The application is anachronistic, but the spirit of his reasoning still echoes in American churches and homes. Among women's groups it is a popular standard for Christian wives, even though only four verses (22–24, 33) speak of a woman's subjection to her husband while nine (25–33) speak of a man's love for his wife.

Paul's main point is usually disregarded. Whereas woman's subordination to man's headship is supported by analogy with Christ and the church, the headship of Christ was not the "authoritarian" rule normally relegated to the husband. Christ's *exousia* was a confusing reversal of mankind's conception of power. The Jews were awaiting a Messiah who would appear with an external kingship; instead He came with an offer of an internal "rule of love."

All of the human relationships which when combined create a society can be boiled down to one constant, according to S. F. Nadel—"mere command differentials."[11] Older sisters control younger brothers, husbands control wives, bosses control workers, and presidents control countries. The ruling one can afford the luxury of kindness because this outward generosity is based on a capacity to exercise violent power. Even the most despotic tyrants call themselves "benefactors" (Luke 22:25). Christ reminded His disciples of this heathen way of solving the authority problem when they tried to set up their own pecking order. And He added that if any of them wished to be the greatest,

---

10. Quoted in Karl Braune, *The Epistle of Paul to the Ephesians*, in CHS, 11:205. The quote continues: ". . . the question assumes a slightly different phase in regard to unmarried women of full age. Still even in the case of such, the passage at least lays the *onus probandi* on those who advocate the right. One popular argument urged in favor of 'woman suffrage' is that thus drunkenness could be stopped by force of law. But . . . the question fairly arises how many men are driven to drunkenness by the failure of their wives to heed the spirit of the Apostle's words."

11. *The Theory of Social Structure* (Glencoe, Ill.: Free, 1957). Quoted in Pike, *With Heart and Mind,* p. 114.

he would have to serve rather than be served (Luke 22:26f; cf. Mark 10:42ff).

These contrary concepts of greatness illustrate the difference between the "lordship" (Gen. 3:16) that characterizes the sinful order[12] and that which is presented in Ephesians 5—a paradoxical authority that contains a self-destruct. If Christ's steps are honestly followed (I Peter 2:21; cf. Eph. 5, the emphatic *kai* in verse 25 and the *houtōs kai* in verse 28, referring back to verses 25ff), then, in the words of Karl Braune,[13] "in one sense every man must die for his wife; he must die to himself, to his sinful Ego, mortify his selfishness and egotism." This concept of love would make the normal marriage relationship almost unrecognizable. In the order of creation, woman was made for man (I Cor. 11:9), even as the church was prepared for Christ; yet as Christ gave Himself to His bride, "not to be served but to serve" (Mark 10:45), so should a man expend himself for his wife. As Christ honored us as "fellow heirs" with Him (Rom. 8:17), so Peter commanded men to "honor" their wives since both of them are "joint heirs of the grace of life" (I Peter 3:7; cf. Gal. 3:28).

In rabbinic thinking, giving honor and respect went one way—up. It was usual for those of higher authority to have little more than disdain for those beneath them. In Ephesians 5:29 Paul implied that husbands even had a propensity to hate their wives—not unnatural since women had little more than physical and monetary value. Socially and politically the woman was indeed the "weaker vessel" (I Peter 3:7),[14] the one who was not honored (Paul, too, consistently used the word "weaker" in this sense, especially in his letters to the Corinthians).[15] Yet, in I Thessa-

---

12. Even Sarah's "lord" (I Peter 3:6) used her in a cowardly way in his attempt to deceive Abimelech.

13. Braune, *Ephesians*, loc. cit.

14. In-depth study of *asthenēs, astheneō,* and *astheneia* reveals that the root meaning is "powerlessness," whether in a physical sense (especially in the Gospels) or in a spiritual sense (as, for example, in I Cor. 8). Perhaps the most revealing use of the adjective is in Romans 5:6, where we read that "Christ died for the ungodly" while we were still "helpless" (NASB), "without strength" (KJV), "powerless to help ourselves" (Knox).

15. See I Corinthians 1:25, where the context (vv. 23–29) shows that "weak" is the same as "base, despised, without boast." The word appears in similar fashion in 4:10, where it means "undistinguished, without honor." Compare 2:3; 11:21, 29; 12:10; 13:3f, 9; 15:43 (where

lonians 4:4f, Paul commanded husbands to treat their wives[16] "in holiness and honor," not just as sexual beings. The two are to meet on a plane of unity and mutuality (I Cor. 7:3–5). They "desire" each other (cf. Gen. 3:16 with Song of Sol. 7:10), they are mutually "indebted" *(apodidotō)* to each other (I Cor. 7:3), they refuse to "defraud" *(apostereite)* one another, they each control *(exousiadzei)* the other's body (v. 4), and decisions are made by mutual consent *(symphōnou,* v. 5). This is a far cry from the Jewish myth about Lilith, the first mate God provided for Adam.

> Adam and Lilith never found peace together; for when he wished to lie with her, she took offence at the recumbent posture he demanded. "Why must I lie beneath you?" she asked. "I also was made from dust, and am therefore your equal." Because Adam tried to compel her obedience by force, Lilith, in a rage, uttered the magic name of God, rose into the air and left him.[17]

Paul's own basis for advocating a male-female relationship of mutual respect was the account of creation found in Genesis 2:21–24. In Ephesians 5:28–33 he elaborated on the implications of the "one flesh" of Adam and Eve. A Christian man is not to treat his wife as if she were a different kind of person, condescending to her, but to love her as if she were himself,[18] to consider the two of them as one body, for in the Lord "neither 'man' nor 'woman' has any separate existence" (I Cor. 11:11 *Phillips*). Charles Williams, considering such passages as Romans 14:7

---

"weakness" is paralleled with "dishonor"); and II Corinthians 11:30; 12:5, 9f; 13:4. Only cultural prejudice and habit can substantiate an interpretation of I Peter 3:7 as "physically weaker," especially since the woman's "honor" is what was at stake.

16. Sylvanus was probably the *amanuensis* ("secretary-scribe") for both I Thessalonians (1:1) and I Peter (5:12), increasing the probability that *skeuos* ("vessel") in I Thessalonians 4:4 does refer to the wife (as in I Peter 3:7); and since "body" in Paul's writings normally refers to the whole person (cf. Rom. 12:1), so "vessel" includes the whole personality of the wife.

17. *Numeri Rabba.* Quoted in Eva Figes, *Patriarchal Attitudes* (New York: Fawcett, 1970), p. 24. This midrash on Numbers was compiled in the twelfth century.

18. Remarkably, this is echoed in a later tractate on marriage in the Babylonian Mishnah, where the husband is told to "love his wife as himself, and honour her more than himself." Quoted in TWNT, 1:361.

("None of us lives for himself. . . ."), Luke 6:31 (the Golden Rule), the great commandment to "love your neighbor as yourself" (Gal. 5:14 et al.) and Ephesians 4:15 (we should grow into one body, with Christ as the head), dealt with the theological principle of mutual dependence and reciprocity.[19] Paul stated it explicitly at the very outset of the Ephesians 5 passage: "Be subject to one another out of reverence for Christ" (5:21 RSV, NEB). Careful examination indicates that Paul's foremost purpose was not to define male-female roles, "nor even to state the duties of husband and wife, but to point out the opportunities for practicing submission in Jesus Christ which were provided by married life at that time."[20]

Submission is "the opposite of self-assertion, of an independent autocratic spirit. It is the desire to get along with one another, being satisfied with less than one's due,"[21] and it should be the attitude of all Christians, female and male. It is surprising how many commentators suggest that Ephesians 5:21 is defined by the subsequent passage, 5:22–6:9, and therefore that its application is confined to wives, children, and slaves. Yet the logical conclusion of that idea would be that the commandment for Christians to "love one another" applies, on the example of Ephesians 5, only to husbands! Whether we talk in terms of *submission* or *love* (in Christ's life the two words became synonymous), the fact remains that we are all to have the *same* care for one another (John 13:14, 34f; Gal. 5:13; Rom. 12:5, 16; 15:5; I Cor. 12:25ff; Eph. 4:25; Rom. 14:19; Phil. 2:3), to "outdo one another in showing honor" (Rom. 12:10).[22]

19. See, for example, Mary McDermott Shideler, *The Theology of Romantic Love: A Study in the Writings of Charles Williams* (Grand Rapids: Eerdmans, 1962), especially chap. 8, "The Way of Exchange," pp. 139–76.

20. Francine Dumas, *Man and Woman: Similarity and Difference,* p. 29.

21. Kenneth S. Wuest, *Ephesians and Colossians in the Greek New Testament* (Grand Rapids: Eerdmans, 1953), p. 129. J. B. Phillips translated Ephesians 5:21 as "fit in with" one another. Billy Graham called it "adapting" to one another, though in all of his writings on the subject, there is hardly a word about how a man is to "adapt" to his wife.

22. *Allēlois* ("one another") in Ephesians 5:21 is unequivocally a *reciprocal* pronoun (no one would limit its use in Matt. 24:10; 25:32; Mark 9:50; Luke 23:12; Acts 19:38; 21:5; Rom. 1:12; 14:13; 15:14; 16:16; Gal. 5:26; Eph. 4:32; Col. 3:9; I Thess. 5:11, 15; James 4:11;

Paul's teaching on submission as exemplified in the husband-wife relationship is within the larger context of Ephesians 4 and 5, in which Paul sought to define Christians *vis-a-vis* pagans, who are "alienated from the life of God because of the ignorance that is in them, due to their hardness of heart" (4:18). He instructed Christians not to be "foolish" *(aphronēs)* but rather to have the mind *(phroneō)* of Christ (Phil. 2:5), who took "the form of a servant . . . [and] humbled himself, and became obedient unto death" (Phil. 2:7f KJV, RSV). Likewise, all Christians are "in humility [to] count others better than themselves" *(tapeinophrosynēi allēlous,* Phil. 2:3; cf. Eph. 5:21). In humility and love we are all, male and female alike, to maintain peace and unity (Eph. 4:1ff; Col. 3:12ff).

A husband and wife being concerned for the rights of each other (Phil. 2:4) is radical even in our present day of enlightenment, going far beyond the feminist demands for independence. For Paul at that time to ask both the stronger and the weaker members of society to bow to each other was unbelievable. In the words of Joseph M. Gettys,[23] "If he did not seem to go far enough, let it be remembered that he went much farther than society as a whole would then sanction" and, we would add, farther than much of today's society would sanction. The implications of "no male and female in Christ" take the grip out of wedlock and free human beings to develop their individual potentials, nourished by an ongoing relationship with Christ.

---

5:9, 16; I Peter 4:9; or anywhere else that personal relations are involved).

23. *How to Study Ephesians* (Richmond: Knox, 1954), p. 52.

# Tensions Between the Old and the New     4

We have applauded Paul's radicalism in his letter to the Ephesians, but when we see more of the existing situations in which women, slaves, and Gentiles were expected to apply his principles, it is all we can do to keep from agreeing with some of his contemporaries who advocated revolution within the ranks. But God's way is loving. When we make "love" instead of new rules, the old regulations are dissolved because they become meaningless, and then there is no necessity forcibly to tear down the social structures that engender them. Only by bearing this in mind can we understand Paul's remaining statements about women and other disenfranchised people.

In a long passage on marriage (I Cor. 7), at the end of a parenthetical discussion on slavery, Paul stated his operational principle for resolving the tensions between the old and the new orders: "My brothers, let every one of us continue to live his life with God in the state in which he was when he was called" (v. 24 *Phillips*). When Paul addressed Jews, masters, and men, he spelled out his vision in bold terms, but Gentiles, slaves, and women he cautioned against a too zealous exercise of Christian freedom. The more he saw this freedom abused, the more he clamped down. This does not make him a thoughtless defender of the status quo; he had good reasons for toning down their deserved freedoms. For one, Paul had constantly to deal with "enthusiasts" who lived as if Christ had destroyed completely the kingdom of this world and had therefore made it a force that no longer needed to be reckoned with. At the same time he himself anticipated an imminent return of Christ with His kingdom (cf. I Cor. 7:25ff) and so, for lack of time, did not try to implement societal change. But his foremost concern was the credibility of the gospel.

Paul advocated total freedom with the provision that each Christian decide how to use it in relation to non-Christians (the NEB heading for I Corinthians 7–11 is "The Christian in a Pagan Society") and that it never become a "cloak" for "maliciousness" (I Peter 2:16 KJV). Since "all things are lawful" (I Cor. 10:23) to a Christian, an action can only be evil inasmuch as it adversely affects another person (Rom. 14:16).

Paul realized there were any number of ways that the total exercise of Christian freedom might bring the gospel into disrepute (I Tim. 6:1). On a one-to-one basis Christians were not to argue, to dispute over words in order to gain prestige (I Tim. 6:1-10), to be quarrelsome (II Tim. 2:24f). They were not to be indecent or disorderly (I Cor. 14:40; Rom. 13:1ff; I Tim. 2:2; Titus 1:5f; 3:1) within their groups or in relation to authorities. And they were not to be insubordinate (I Tim. 6:1–5) within the social institutions to which they belonged (slavery, wifehood, etc.). Rather, they were to practice "godliness with contentment" (I Tim. 6:6). This meant forgetting their own advantages in order to fulfill the needs of others (Gal. 5:13–6:5; I Cor. 8:7–9:23; 10:23–33; cf. Rom. 13:5 and I Tim. 1:19 on "conscience"). A lack of love would only prove that their freedom was a semblance.

As a result of his concern that all Christians present the gospel in its true form, Paul spoke sharply to the subjected one to curtail newly discovered freedom. At the Jerusalem council (Acts 15) he declared the equal status of the Gentiles and the Jews, but then he urged the former to subscribe to the Jewish laws that required abstinence from idol-meat, from blood, from things strangled, and from fornication.[1] The reason he gave was that they should

---

1. It was also at this council (Acts 15:1f; Gal. 2:1ff) that Paul refused

not upset the common practice (v. 21) of the synagogue churches (the error of the antinomian Nicolaitans in the Ephesian church in later years [Rev. 2:1–7] was their practice of eating meat sacrificed to idols). None of these practices in themselves bothered Paul (cf. I Cor. 8:7ff), but he was concerned that the "strong" (in this case the Gentiles who came to Christ apart from the law and who were boasting in their libertine stance) not offend the "weak" (here the Jews who discovered Christ from a religious adherence to the laws). The principle of freedom had to be subordinated to the principle of love.

Similarly, the "slave who is called to life in Christ is set free in the eyes of the Lord" (I Cor. 7:22 *Phillips;* cf. Gal. 3:28). But in order not to cause disorder the slave is to use his or her situation as an opportunity to serve others (I Tim. 6:1f), not just out of obedience to the laws of slavery—that is the *old* way—but wholeheartedly (Col. 3:23), "out of reverence for the Lord" (v. 22 NEB), who is Himself above all rulers.

There is a continuing dispute over I Corinthians 7:21, whether it ought to be translated: "If, besides" *(ei kai),* you are offered freedom, then "choose" *(chrēsai)* to be free; or "even if" *(ei kai)* you have the offer, "make use" *(chrēsai)* of your servitude. According to Arthur P. Stanley this is "one of the most evenly balanced questions in the interpretation of the New Testament."[2] The first translation is favored by John Calvin and most commentators since the Reformation; the other, by Martin Luther and most commentators before the Reformation. On the basis of grammar *(ei kai* is nearly always concessive; cf. *all'* ... *mallon,* "But ... rather," both here and in I Timothy 6:2) and context (freedom in Christ is given as the *reason* [*gar,* v. 22] for using the position of a slave as an opportunity to share Christ's love), we choose the second reading. The best translation of verse 21 is in the NEB margin:

---

to circumcise Titus, who was Gentile by birth. But when he chose Timothy to accompany him on his second tour (Acts 16:1–3), Paul was willing to have him circumcised, to conciliate the Jewish Christians (16:3). Timothy's mother, Eunice, who became a Christian on Paul's first tour (16:1), was a Jew (16:3; II Tim. 1:5), while his father was a Greek (16:1, 3) who probably objected to Timothy's being circumcised in infancy.

2. Quoted in Christian Friedrich Kling, *The First Epistle to the Corinthians,* in CHS, 10:153.

"Even if a chance of liberty should come, choose rather to make good use of your servitude."

When we reconsider Philemon and Onesimus and remember that Paul asked Philemon to face Onesimus, we find that Paul, because he spoke to the one in control of the slave, was still operating on a basis of love. Only a master had the opportunity to destroy a master-slave relationship and at the same time maintain peace and love. Were a slave to take the initiative, he or she risked immediate anarchy and would contribute little to changing the institution of slavery as a whole.

If Paul stepped lightly on the issues of Gentiles and slaves, when it came to women it would seem he exercised undue caution (in I Corinthians 12:13 and Colossians 3:11 the male/female couplet is conspicuous by its absence). However, for him to have advocated social and political changes in sexual relationships would have distracted his converts from the central message of the gospel—mutual subjection out of love for Christ.

We will now look at the passages about women wearing a veil, speaking in tongues, teaching, and bearing children. Each area presents another aspect of subjection, which is related to the extraordinarily low status of the female within the cultural milieu that Paul was acquainted with and which must be seen as one means of preserving peace and thus showing God's love. *Without* this understanding the passages become outdated prescriptions that when applied today, hamstring Christian women and turn non-Christians away from the Bible. *With* this understanding we can see that Paul recognized the freedom (power) that females have in Christ and asked them to apply it by voluntarily subjecting themselves so they might remain free, even within the most repressive relationships.

A *"What If ..."* cartoon in *Christianity Today* (14 April 1972) showed Paul arriving in Corinth, seeing angry women with signs reading "Women of Corinth unite" and "Paul the apostle is a male chauvinist pig," and saying to them, "I see you received my letter." It is difficult to reconstruct the precise nature of the problems that Paul faced in Corinth, but it is highly unlikely that one was a city-wide movement for the emancipation of women.[3] The women's liberation movement seems to have been among the Chris-

---

3. J. A. Fitzmyer, "A Feature of Qumran Angelology and the Angels of I Cor. 11:10," *New Testament Studies* 4 (1957): 48 (n. 2).

tians themselves, who rejected common ecclesiastical practice concerning the veil in favor of Corinthian customs (cf. 11:2, 16).

The churches had taken over the Jewish attitude that for a married woman not to cover her head in worship symbolized her rebellion against God and her husband. But married Greek women, accustomed to wearing veils both in their homes and on the streets of Corinth, commonly removed them during religious assemblies. To further complicate matters, Corinth was a notorious hotbed of sin, its reputation substantiated by its temple of Aphrodite and the accompanying one thousand sacred prostitutes,[4] who not only symbolized their status by never wearing a veil but were, with slaves, forbidden to wear one on pain of torture[5] (see Numbers 5:18 and Genesis 24:65ff for similar attitudes in Jewish culture). It is possible, then, that Paul's purpose was not only to differentiate the conduct of Christian women in their assemblies from that of the Corinthian idol worshipers, but also to avoid their being identified with the temple "virgins" themselves. Already there was wild talk among the populace about activities at Christian "love feasts," and Paul astutely sought to prevent the churches from misrepresenting themselves.

From this perspective the Aramaic pun of I Corinthians 11:10 (*exousia/kalumma; see* above) assumes yet another level of meaning. The Christian woman was liberated; she had *exousia.* But in the same letter, when Paul discussed idols and Christian freedom, he warned, ". . . take heed lest by any means this liberty [*exousia*] of yours become a stumblingblock to them that are weak" (8:9 KJV). So in Corinth the *exousia* on her head was literally protected by the *kalumma* she wore in worship (cf. I Peter 2:16, where the admonition is against using "your freedom as a pretext [*epikalumma*] for evil") and that "because of the angels."[6]

---

4. Friedrich Hauck and Siegfried Schulz, in TWNT, 6:582.

5. Eugenie Andruss Leonard, "St. Paul on the Status of Women," *Catholic Biblical Quarterly* 12 (1950): 317ff.

6. See G. G. Findlay, *St. Paul's First Epistle to the Corinthians,* in EGT, 2:874. According to Findlay, the angels "present in Divine worship" are "offended by . . . misconduct" (cf. I Tim. 5:21). In Daniel and other Jewish writings, the angels are presented as guardians of good manners. Paul himself seemed concerned about what they observed (I Cor. 4:9; cf. I Peter 1:12). There is Biblical evidence of the involvement of angels with law and order. They were at Mount Sinai (Gal. 3:19; Ps. 68:17; Exod. 3:2; Acts 7:38); they may have been present at

Another "shocking" (*aischron*, I Cor. 14:35 NEB) matter in the Corinthian church was the verbal participation of females in their religious gatherings (many today would agree with J. B. Phillips that "there is something indecorous about a woman's speaking in Church"). Chloe (I Cor. 1:11), according to Eugenie Andruss Leonard,[7] was a highborn woman who may have complained to Paul about the shameful rantings of undisciplined Christian women from the lower castes, including former harlots and mistresses (*hetairae*). Whatever the immediate reason, Paul left no doubt in the minds of the congregation that women were to "veil" themselves with silence:

> ... the women should keep silence in the churches. For they are not permitted to speak, but should be subordinate, as even the law says. If there is anything they desire to know, let them ask their husbands at home, for it is shameful for a woman to speak in church (14:34f).

A similar statement is found in his letter to Timothy in Ephesus:

> Let a woman learn in silence with all submissiveness. I permit no woman to teach or to have authority over men; she is to keep silent (I Tim. 2:11f).

The slight differences between these two passages are compounded by a third: "Any woman who prays or prophesies with her head unveiled dishonors her head" (I Cor. 11:5), which assumes that women did in fact pray and prophesy (cf. 11:13; women, like men, were probably "not lacking in any spiritual gift," 1:7). The problem is not resolved by referring the statements in chapter 14 to church behavior (cf. I Tim. 2:8, *en panti topōi*, a reference to all the "home churches" in Ephesus) and those in 11:5 to public behavior, because 11:2–16 just as clearly pertains to worship in the *ekklēsia* ("church"). A possibility exists that women were not allowed to "talk" in public church meetings but were allowed to "prophesy" in private assemblies attended only by believers, but this disregards the fact that Paul based most of the guidelines

creation ("According to one ancient midrash, ... when God said, 'Let us make man,' he was addressing the angels," reported Fitzmyer ["The Angels of I Cor. 11:10," p. 55]); and they are often associated by Paul with the "principalities and powers" that govern this world, that maintain its order and smooth operation.

7. "The Status of Women," p. 318.

in both chapters on common practice in all the churches (11:16; 14:33[34]; cf. 7:17). We believe the context of chapter 14 provides a better solution.

Some ancient manuscripts have placed verses 34–35 after verse 40, indicating the scribes' inability to see the connection between the "women" verses and the remainder of the chapter, but their very desire to preserve the unity of the passage is strong evidence that Paul, while speaking on "tongues," was in some way led to this exhortation to women. It is for us to find that connection, and our clue is in the word *laleō* ("to speak"), which occurs in both verses 34 and 35 and two dozen times in this one chapter, usually in connection with *glōssai* ("tongues").

One of Paul's main points was that "speaking in tongues" is not that valuable to the congregation, and he gave two reasons: (1) it edifies only the speaker, not the group (vv. 2ff); and (2) it is a "sign" not to believers, who do not need it, but to unbelievers (v. 22), even though the latter still may choose not to believe (v. 23; cf. v. 21). Paul continued to rail against excess and disorder. Whether through "speaking in tongues" (vv. 27f) or "prophesying" (vv. 29ff), if "confusion" reigned (v. 33), then it was better to have "silence" (vv. 28, 30). Surely this was the context for his command that "women should keep silence in the churches" (v. 34 RSV; the same *sigaō* is used all three times).

In verse 34, women's silence is set in opposition to their wanting to learn; it follows that their "speaking" was linked to their "ignorance." We assume that women were "speaking" in tongues, and this coincides with 11:5, that women were "praying and prophesying" (Paul used *laleō* in 14:29 to refer to "prophesying," but his emphasis in the chapter was on tongues; cf. verse 14, which speaks of praying "in a tongue"). But evidently the bulk of their "speaking" was unprofitable. Paul reminded everyone that "he who speaks in a tongue should pray for the power to interpret. For if I pray in a tongue, my spirit prays but my mind is unfruitful" (vv. 13f), demonstrating that the one "speaking" was too often unaware of what he or she said. Paul forbade no one, male or female (14:39; 11:5), to prophesy or to speak in tongues, unless it resulted in disorder or confusion. And one way to eliminate half the chaos was to invoke the "law" (v. 34) that women were to be excluded from prayer (cf. *andras*, "males," in I Tim. 2:8 and *hēsuchia*, "silence," of the women in vv. 11f). Paul justified this decision not on spiritual grounds but out of expedience. For whether a man or woman claimed to be "a prophet, or spiritual" (that is, worshiped God in a tongue), that person should remember that even this claim was superceded by Paul's "command of the Lord" (v. 37)—peace should reign in the congregation of God.

There was no peace when women taught in the congregation because this was completely foreign to Jewish customs. In the synagogues of Ephesus, as elsewhere, women as a rule did not speak, and rabbinic prohibitions even ruled out a mother's teaching the Torah to her own children. Such regulations probably account for Paul's failure to mention women in his rehearsal (I Cor. 15:5ff) of those who saw the risen Lord, for, as F. F. Bruce pointed out, "Outside Christian circles, the evidence of women would have been dismissed as of little value. Had it been added, it would have been ridiculed as the fantasies of excitable females."[8] Celsus raised this very objection in the second century, and the apostles themselves reacted similarly to the women's tale, which seemed to them "sheer imagination" (Luke 24:11 Phillips).

It did not disturb Paul that women were participating equally with men; he was worried about the implications of the teaching itself (it should be noted that the Greek of I Timothy 2:12 emphasizes "teach" rather than "women"). Any woman who possessed full knowledge and could express it (I Cor. 1:5 NEB) he accepted wholeheartedly as a fellow teacher (didaskein is the word used in both Acts 18:25 and I Timothy 2:12). Any Christian could come to the truth and be able to share it (I Cor. 1:5ff; Col. 3:16; cf. Eph. 5:8–17), but at the same time any Christian could also depart from the truth and lead others astray. Many commentators assume Eve's deception (I Tim. 2:14) and her teaching the man (Gen. 3:17, he "hearkened" to her) to be fatal for all time, and as a result men must constantly be on guard against all women—who are just like Eve. They substantiate their fear by referring to John's words to the church in Thyatira (Rev. 2:20): "I have this against you, that you tolerate the woman Jezebel, who calls herself a prophetess and is teaching and beguiling

---

8. The Dawn of Christianity (London: Paternoster, 1950). Quoted in Charles C. Ryrie, The Place of Women in the Church, p. 37.

my servants to practice immorality and to eat food sacrificed to idols." But they fail to notice that in II Corinthians 11:3 Eve's foolishness serves as a negative model for the whole church, not just for the women. And Titus 1:10ff presents a case of ignorant (probably male) teachers who should "shut up" (v. 11; *epistomidzein,* used only here in the New Testament, is much stronger than the *hēsuchia* of I Timothy 2:11f). It would seem that Paul was not so anxious to protect men from subversive females as he was to protect the gospel from false teaching.

A major problem among the early Christians was the inability of many to discern truth from falsehood. Women's social position placed them squarely in this category of "weaker vessel" (I Peter 3:7), their actual intellectual position being that of a child (cf. Eph. 4:13f; this situation colored Paul's teaching about widows, "free women" under sixty [I Tim. 5:9ff], who were likely to be enslaved by more than one vice [Titus 2:3]). In his second letter to Timothy (3:6f), he was especially solicitous about the weakest of the women, those who were "silly" and easily taken "captive" by false teachers. In Donald Guthrie's words, "These women apparently desire to listen to other people's advice *(ever learning),* but their minds have become so fickle and warped that they have become incapable of attaining the *knowledge of the truth* (cf. I Tim. 2:4)."[9] Related to their general unlearnedness was the women's "indecorously lording it over men."[10] When they domineered (*authentein;* see above) they risked being as disruptive as Eve (I Tim. 2:14). But domineering is not limited to females; it is a concomitant of weakness. The less knowledgeable a person, the more likely she or he is to domineer; whereas the stronger person, because of her or his position, has no need to compensate. After her fall Eve no longer spoke with true understanding. In her weakened state (there is no evidence for the contention that Eve was weaker than Adam before the fall) she probably approached Adam believing the serpent's promise that she would be like a god in her understanding (Gen. 3:5). Likewise, Christian women, in light of their

---

9. *The Pastoral Epistles: An Introduction and Commentary* (Grand Rapids: Eerdmans, 1957), p. 159. Note how women today are taught that they are more easily "led astray" than men, something Paul never says but only accepts as a cultural "given."

10. Ibid., p. 75.

promised *exousia,* would have tried to mask their immaturity by domineering over male church leaders. In summary, Paul's experience led him to distrust weak people to teach or to be in authority, and, given women's undeveloped intellect—undeveloped because of their low social status—it is understandable that he issued a general statement forbidding them to teach.

Woman's social stronghold was the home. The respectable married woman expended all her energies there and deferred on all counts to her husband. And no matter what her new position in relation to God, Christ, or man, the church was already menacing enough to society without threatening the home structure as well. So, as he did slaves and Gentiles, Paul advised women to live as free people within their otherwise stifling cultural bounds.

After effectively silencing the woman in the church he continued (I Tim. 2:15), ". . . she shall be saved in childbearing, if they continue in faith and charity and holiness with sobriety" (KJV). Paul seems to have been offering women the hope that "the original curse upon their race is mitigated by Christian salvation,"[11] that in spite of the curse she shall be saved. But this raises several problems. First, who are the "she" and "they" in the verse? It is very difficult to prove that "she" refers to either Eve or Mary. It probably refers to Christian wives in general; the plural "they" then refers to the "women" of verses 9f. The disastrous suggestion that "they" indicates children makes the mother's salvation depend on her children's actions, an impossible view. Neither was Paul presenting motherhood as penance for woman's original sin, nor as any basis for salvation. The latter is impossible because the women to whom Paul was writing were already Christians. I Corinthians 7 is additional proof that Paul did not believe a woman's salvation depends on bearing children, and it also makes improbable Joachim Jeremias's thought "that the duty of child-bearing is emphasized to offset the unnatural abstinence advocated by false teachers."[12] What is missing in all these unsubstantial attempts to elucidate I Timothy 2:15 is that childbearing is *not* the issue but is only a *condition (dia)*[13] in which she can find

---

11. Ibid., p. 78.

12. Ibid.

13. *Dia* is used in several ways with the genitive, one of which implies attendant circumstances or environment, or, as Friedrich W.

The Old and the New

blessing. We must also reject Phillips's translation, "that women will come safely through childbirth," unless we mean no more than we would by saying "men will come safely through gardening."[14] For, as B. D. Glass pointed out, woman's "pain" (Gen. 3:16) and man's "toil" (v. 17) translate the same Hebrew word, *itstsabon*.[15] What should have been translated "labor" or "hard work" in both verses instead was rendered according to the prejudice of KJV, RSV, and other translators. Likewise *etzev*, the second word translated "pain" in Genesis 3:16, was a common term for labor and was so translated elsewhere, as in Genesis 5:29 and Proverbs 14:23. The verse in Proverbs, "In all labour there is profit," is the concept Paul sought to apply to the female's "vocation" in I Timothy 2:15.

Woman's profit, "she will be *saved*," is best understood as "her attitude will be a *healthy* one" or "she will be a *whole person*" in motherhood.[16] But her "salvation" is derived not from childbearing itself; it is clearly (cf. *ean*, "if") a result of faith, love, holiness, and common sense. To "obey the rules" of motherhood because that is a "woman's place" is to live according to the gospel. Paul also urged younger women to remain in their female world by marrying and bearing children, so they would "give no opponent occasion for slander" (I Tim. 5:14 NEB; in Phillips's words, "They should certainly not be the means of lowering the reputation of the Church, although some, alas, have already played into the enemy's hands," vv. 14f). They should be "workers at home" (*oikourgous*),

---

Blass and A. de Brunner put it, "circumstances in which one finds oneself because of something." *Greek Grammar of the New Testament and Other Early Christian Literature* (Chicago: University of Chicago, 1961), p. 119. It is so used in II Corinthians 2:4 (he cried as he wrote) and probably in I Peter 3:20 (they were saved "in the flood" [*Phillips*] or "as they passed through the waves" [*Knox*]).

14. Clara Bewick Colby came to the point: "For Adam, not Eve, the earth was to bring forth the thorn and the thistle, and he was to eat his bread by the sweat of his brow. Yet I never heard a sermon on the sin of uprooting weeds.... It is when she tries to lighten her load that the world is afraid of sacrilege and the overthrow of nature." In WB, 2:37.

15. Quoted in Grantly Dick-Read, *Childbirth Without Fear: The Principles and Practice of Natural Childbirth,* 2nd ed. (New York: Harper and Row, 1953), pp. 96f.

16. Cf. n. 2 of chap. 3 on the meaning of the Greek word for salvation.

"that the word of God be not blasphemed" (Titus 2:5 KJV). Whereas non-Christians might be intimidated by audacious women, they would not be put off by those who were sober, reasonable, self-controlled (*sōphrosunē*, I Tim. 2:15, also v. 9). It was Paul's prayer (I Tim. 2:2) that all Christians, male and female, might "lead a quiet and peaceable life" (*hēsuchion bion;* cf. v. 12, *hēsuchiai*, and I Peter 3:4, *hēsuchiou pneumatos*), being "godly" (*eusebeiai;* cf. *theosebeian* in v. 10) "and respectful" (*semnotēti*). He opposed contention with all his heart and preached a "gospel of peace" (Rom. 10:15 KJV). For Paul, to fulfill one's "duties" is to apply the principle of peace.

Not only feminists have been disturbed by Paul's commands for women to "keep their place" (I Cor. 14:34 NEB), to be submissive to their husbands. Even Pope Pius XI (*Casti Connubii*, 31 December 1930) hedged on the import of *hypotassō* ("submit, be subject") with the following doubletalk: "Woman is not to live in subjection but in devotion to the good of the home." But it is unassailable that *hypotassō* denotes inferior rank (it was originally a military term and is often used in the papyri in the sense of an "appendage" to documents), that "to submit" and "to obey" are practically synonymous (Titus 3:1; Heb. 13:17), and that in the New Testament "submission" does not depend on the character of the authority.[17] Paul's use of such a forceful word as *hypotassō* in the woman passages makes willing antifeminists of most men and reluctant ones of many women.

Those who embrace this conservative reading of *hypotassō* and those to whom it is a stumblingblock both subject Paul's teaching to error, in two respects. First, they too often ignore the purpose of submission—to preserve peace. A married woman is to do her "duty" (*hōs anēken*, Col. 3:18), she is to do what is "becoming," in order that Christ's peace may rule the home. Conflict will thus be sidestepped, an unbelieving spouse may be "sanctified" (I Cor. 7:14), and her fear of her husband will dissolve— by giving herself to him she will make impotent his power over her. Despite her "lord's" (Abraham's) misuse of her,

---

17. The prime example of this is Ephesians 5:24 where, though the analogy between man and Christ breaks down because of the latter's being the "savior of the body," a strong *alla* ("nevertheless") indicates that the parallel still holds in the realm of submission, that women are to be subject to their husbands "in everything."

Sarah the "freewoman" (Gal. 4:22f), by her submission to him, negated all "terror" of his authority over her (I Peter 3:6; cf. Rom. 13:3). Without fear she was free to love him (cf. I John 4:18).

Second, those who emphasize Paul's teaching on woman's submission overlook the fact that for him submission is a universal principle, applicable to all Christians, that it did not make females and males different kinds of people, and that each is to be subject to the other—not because of the other's "place" but because of reverence for Christ. Paul and the other apostles commanded submission not so much in the context of society's law, necessary to restrain the destructive impulses of sinful people, as in the context of the new order of love, which made "free people" even of those whom society considered bound.

# Conclusion                                    5

Paul knew that power could only be shared by the one who controlled it, and if it were not shared in love, it was frequently fought over. So he did not counsel women to seek control in the churches; he, a male, shared his own authority with them. The New Testament mentions many qualified women whom Paul encountered in his ministry. Among them were two to whom he entrusted major responsibility—Phoebe and Prisca. So George Bernard Shaw's statement that "Paul was a rash and not very deep man, as his contempt for women shews" cannot be true; by recognizing women as his equals Paul could show them no contempt. He was a wise and very deep man, as the honor he showed these women proves beyond doubt.

The position of Phoebe and Prisca is in opposition to the traditional view of Paul's teaching—that a female is inferior to a male in every sense except the spiritual, that the male should rule over her, and that to please God she should subject herself to that rule.

The feminists accept the traditional interpretation but they reject its implications. They favor legislation that would limit the authority of males and increase that of females.

We submit that Paul was no respecter of persons, that he was a radical who went beyond both the traditionalists and the feminists by preaching mutual submission for the sake of Christ, and that his application of this principle was colored by his culture, both pagan and Jewish.

The old orders were characterized by the law and came about as a result of Eve's and Adam's sin. Traditional commentators have based their view of woman's subjection on the rabbinic interpretation of the orders of creation (woman was created after man and hence is inferior to him) and transgression (she sinned first and so is inferior).

We acknowledge that Eve was created second but do not consider this sufficient cause for her subjection, since both she and man were created in God's image and both in their worship have direct access to Him. Eve, weakened by her sin, usurped God's authority over Adam, and he sinned. God's curse broke their unity with Him and with each other, and the law codified the differences between them. But Christ's coming broke down all the rules and regulations, including the Jews' privileged position, the masters' control, and the males' authority over females (Gal. 3:28).

No longer was only the weaker to submit to the stronger, but each was to submit to the other out of love for Christ, who by making Himself the lowest became the highest.

While we favor the results of reforms and of the self-consciousness of the women's lib movement, we do not believe that the application of their principles, without mutual submission, will alleviate the tyrannies they hope to overthrow. Their writings continue to make us conscious of inequalities both inside and outside marriage relationships. But in order for it to grow, increasing consciousness must be accompanied by a like commitment to serve each other in Christ's peace.

We have to face *all* the injustices our male-dominated society engenders. That means discrimination in defining our jobs (housewives and students both "work" even though they are not paid for it), on the job (female bosses are not inherently less capable than their male counterparts), in the home (males are not naturally less "maternal" than females), in the church (Sunday school leaflets for two-year-olds portray little boys as troublemakers and little girls as Mama's helpers), and on the street (when was the last time you read that a man was raped by a woman or saw a female wolf-whistle at a male?).

We have to acknowledge that Christians often condone discrimination in the "home" and refuse to see it in "society" (including the church), while liberationists never stop fighting it. But neither have the solution. Those Christians who are in power—males—must take away the feminists' cause by recognizing and abolishing the injustices where they begin—with themselves.

# Annotated
# Bibliography

Though somewhat broader in focus than the book, this bibliography reflects the book's orientation in that although it includes historical and other material, it concentrates primarily on the question of the Biblical (especially the Pauline) view of women; in that while including material from a variety of positions, it gravitates toward writings arguing for the equality of women to men and their full participation in church life; and in that while a variety of theological positions are represented, it is weighted toward those in the more conservative spectrum.

The literature on this question is so extensive that any bibliography must of necessity be very selective. Those wishing further help might move in several directions. The most accessible related bibliography is by Charles Edward Cerling, Jr., "An Annotated Bibliography of the New Testament Teaching About Women," *Journal of the Evangelical Theological Society* 16 (1973): 47–53. Less accessible but very helpful is a more narrowly focused bibliographical essay by Sakae Kubo, "The Bible and the Ordination of Women," *Spectrum* 7, no. 2 (n.d.): 29–33. Clare Fischer and Rochelle Gatlin have prepared a large and quite general bibliography on "Woman: A Theological

Perspective," available from the Office of Women's Affairs of the Graduate Theological Union in Berkeley, California.

Allworthy, Thomas Bateson. *Women in the Apostolic Church.* Cambridge, Eng.: Heffer, 1917.
Though written over half a century ago, this remains a classic study of the New Testament evidence for the role of women in the early church.

Bailey, Derrick Sherwin. *Sexual Relations in Christian Thought.* New York: Harper, 1959.
Also published as *The Man-Woman Relation in Christian Thought,* this book is a careful historical study of the varieties of Christian teaching on marriage and sexuality. In a final chapter, "Towards a Theology of Sex," the author retracts his defense of the subordination of women in his earlier *The Mystery of Love and Marriage.*

Barth, Markus. *Ephesians.* 2 vols. The Anchor Bible. New York: Doubleday, 1974.
Listed primarily because over 100 pages in the second volume are devoted to interpreting and providing background material for the important passage on marriage in Ephesians 5.

Bedale, Stephen. "The Meaning of *Kephalē* in the Pauline Epistles." *Journal of Theological Studies* 5 (1954): 211–15.
An important little essay arguing that Paul's use of *head* is better understood in terms of "beginning" than "over-lord."

Bliss, Kathleen. *The Service and Status of Women in the Churches.* London: SCM, 1952.
Commissioned by the World Council of Churches and based on a survey of nearly fifty countries, this volume provides much historical and statistical information on the question of women in the church as it stood a quarter of a century ago.

Booth, Catherine. *Female Ministry; or, Woman's Right to Preach the Gospel.* London: Morgan and Chase, 1859.
Catherine Mumford Booth, cofounder with her husband, William, of the Salvation Army, was an ardent feminist largely responsible for the egalitarian convictions of the Army. This booklet was also published as a chapter in *Papers on Practical Religion* and has

recently been reprinted (with some editing) as an inexpensive pamphlet by the New York Publishing Department of the Salvation Army.

Brunner, Peter. *The Ministry and the Ministry of Women.* St. Louis: Concordia, 1971.

This booklet opposes the ordination of women by arguing that it is contrary to the *"kephalē* structure" established in the "orders of creation." Brunner is answered by John Reumann, "What in Scripture Speaks to the Ordination of Women?" *Concordia Theological Monthly* 44 (1973): 5–30.

Bushnell, Katherine C. *God's Word to Women.* Oakland, Calif.: Katherine C. Bushnell, 1923.

Now half a century old, this collection of 100 Bible studies on "woman's place in the divine economy" was authored by a medical missionary and social reformer who devoted her retirement to developing a nonsexist interpretation of the Scriptures. Though based on careful work in the Greek and Hebrew, not all her exegetical conclusions will stand scrutiny, but the book remains an important effort to argue for feminism while maintaining a very conservative view of Scripture. A modern paperback reprint may be obtained from Ray B. Munson, Box 52, North Collins, NY 14111.

Caird, George B. "Paul and Women's Liberty." *Bulletin of the John Rylands Library* 54 (1972): 268–81.

The 1971 Manson Memorial Lecture (University of Manchester) in which a British New Testament scholar argues that Paul was a passionate advocate of liberty.

*Concerning the Ordination of Women.* Geneva: World Council of Churches, 1964.

This volume reprints several papers originally prepared for the Fourth World Conference on Faith and Order (a section of the World Council of Churches) held in Montreal, 1963. Particularly noteworthy is an extended theological and Biblical analysis by Andre Dumas on "Biblical Anthropology and the Participation of Women in the Ministry of the Church."

Danielou, Jean. *The Ministry of Women in the Early Church.* London: Faith, 1961.

In this pamphlet (an English translation of a French article) a Roman Catholic scholar surveys the ministry of women in the New Testament and early-church fathers.

*Daughters of Sarah.*
A bimonthly newsletter from a "Christian feminist perspective" that carries exegetical, historical, theological, and practical articles as well as news and reviews of current literature and happenings. *Daughters of Sarah,* 5104 N. Christiana Ave., Chicago, IL 60625.

Dayton, Donald W., and Dayton, Lucille Sider. "Women as Preachers: Evangelical Precedents." *Christianity Today,* 23 May 1973, pp. 4–7.
A short survey of the surprising amount of feminist conviction and women ministers in earlier years of the evangelical tradition. Further amplification of this material may be found in a chapter entitled "Evangelical Roots of Feminism" in Donald W. Dayton, *Discovering an Evangelical Heritage* (New York: Harper and Row, 1976).

Dumas, Francine. *Man and Woman: Similarity and Difference.* Geneva: World Council of Churches, 1966.
This study, translated from the French, treats sociological, theological, and practical aspects of a wide spectrum of modern questions about sexuality and sex roles.

"Evangelical Feminism." *Post-American* 3 (August-September 1974).
This whole issue was devoted to historical, theological, and Biblical aspects of an emerging "evangelical feminism." It also contains an annotated bibliography by Nancy Hardesty.

Ford, Josephine M. "Biblical Material Relevant to the Ordination of Women." *Journal of Ecumenical Studies* 10 (1973): 669–94.
A prominent Biblical scholar and theologian in the Catholic charismatic renewal movement surveys the relevant Biblical material (especially Pauline) to conclude that there is no Biblical obstacle to the ordination of women. Also available in abridged form as "The Bible and the Ordination of Women," *Theology Digest* 22 (1974): 23–29.

Franson, Fredrik: "Prophesying Daughters." *Covenant Quarterly* 34 (November 1976).
A defense of the evangelistic work of women by the founder of The Evangelical Alliance Mission (TEAM). Franson's impact on the Evangelical Free Church

helped open the way for the ministry of women in that denomination in its early years.

Fraser, David, and Fraser, Elouise. "A Biblical View of Women: Demythologizing Sexegesis." *Theology, News and Notes* 21 (June 1975): 14–18.

Two Fuller Theological Seminary students argue for the "ontological" and "functional" equality of women —grounding their discussion in careful Biblical study. This article is extracted from a larger mimeographed manuscript entitled "A Biblical View of Women" (1974), available from the authors.

Gibson, Elsie. *When the Minister Is a Woman.* New York: Holt, Rinehart, and Winston, 1970.

A minister in the United Church of Christ here reports, in popular and anecdotal style, a survey of women ministers and the problems they face.

Gordon, A. J. "The Ministry of Women." *Missionary Review of the World.* New series, 7 (1894): 910–21.

This exegetical defense of the ministry of women was authored by the founder of Gordon College. It has been repeatedly reprinted: as a pamphlet by the China Inland Mission; as "Gordon-Conwell Monograph No. 61," with an introduction by the Rev. Pamela Cole; and in abridged form in *Theology, News and Notes,* 21 (June 1975).

Hardesty, Nancy. "Women and Evangelical Christianity." In *The Cross and the Flag,* edited by Robert Clouse, Robert Linder, and Richard Pierard. Wheaton: Creation House, 1972.

An early statement of Nancy Hardesty that attempts to outline a basic theological position to support Christian feminism. It is to some extent an amplification of her "Women: Second Class Citizens," *Eternity* 22 (January 1971); in the same issue of *Eternity,* ten evangelical leaders responded to Hardesty's article.

Hooker, Morna D. "Authority on Her Head: An Examination of I Cor. 11:10." *New Testament Studies* 10 (1963–64): 410–16.

An important study of I Corinthians 11:2–16, concluding that what is at stake is women's submission to God, not to men.

Hoppin, Ruth. *Priscilla: Author of the Epistle to the Hebrews.* New York: Exposition, 1969.

The longest essay in this volume is a modern restatement of the arguments to support the claim that Priscilla wrote the Epistle to the Hebrews. See the annotation to Lee Anna Starr, *Bible Status of Women,* for more on this question.

Howard, Thomas, and Dayton, Donald W. "A Dialogue on Women, Hierarchy and Equality." *Post-American* 4 (May 1975): 8–15.

This dialogue between advocates of hierarchical (Howard) and egalitarian (Dayton) views of the relationship between the sexes identifies a number of the historical, theological, and Biblical factors involved in the discussion.

Jewett, Paul K. *Man as Male and Female.* Grand Rapids: Eerdmans, 1975.

A theology professor from Fuller Theological Seminary rethinks the Western theological tradition to argue on Biblical and theological grounds for a fundamentally egalitarian view of the relationship between the sexes.

Knight, George W., III. *The Role Relation of Man and Woman and the Teaching/Ruling Functions in the Church.* St. Louis: George W. Knight, III, 1975.

This booklet, originally an article in the spring 1975 issue of the *Journal of the Evangelical Theological Society,* is a major attack on the emerging Biblical feminist movement. It is available from the author at Covenant Theological Seminary, 12330 Conway Road, St. Louis, MO 63141. Knight has more directly critiqued the work of Jewett, Scanzoni, and Hardesty in "Male and Female Related He Them," *Christianity Today,* 9 April 1976, pp. 13–17.

Lee, Luther. *Woman's Right to Preach the Gospel.* Syracuse, N.Y.: Luther Lee, 1853.

This pamphlet contains the sermon preached by Wesleyan Methodist Luther Lee at the ordination of Congregationalist Antoinette Brown, generally acknowledged to be the first woman fully ordained to the Christian ministry. It defends her ordination on Biblical grounds. A modern edition is available in *Five Sermons and a Tract by Luther Lee,* edited and introduced by Donald W. Dayton, published by Holrad House, 5104 N. Christiana Ave., Chicago, IL 60625.

Leonard, Eugenie Andruss. "St. Paul on the Status of Women." *Catholic Biblical Quarterly* 12 (1950): 311–20.

An overview of the Pauline statements on women and

their historical context that concludes that I Corinthians 14:34–35 and I Timothy 2:11–12 are directed to special situations not universally applicable (such as recently converted harlots playing fast and loose with their new Christian freedom) and that Paul actually sowed the seeds that have come to fruit in the equality of women.

Leslie, William. "The Concept of Woman in the Pauline Corpus in the Light of the Religious and Social Environment of the First Century." Ph.D. dissertation, Northwestern University, 1975.

This lengthy dissertation by the pastor of LaSalle Street Church in Chicago exegetes each of the Pauline texts against a careful study of its historical context and also analyzes the variety of ways in which Paul has been interpreted on this question. Now available only through University Microfilms, Ann Arbor, Michigan, this study is being revised for publication.

Mollenkott, Virginia. *Women, Men, and the Bible.* Nashville: Abingdon, 1977.

The most comprehensive statement of a Milton scholar who has written on the feminist interpretation of the Scriptures. See also her keynote address at the first national conference of the Evangelical Women's Caucus, published as "Women and the Bible: A Challenge to Male Interpretation," *Sojourners* 5 (February 1976): 20–25. Also see "Church Women, Theologians, and the Burden of Proof," *Reformed Journal* 25 (July-August 1975): 18–20 and (September 1975) 17–21; and "The Total Submission Woman," *Christian Herald* 98 (November 1975): 26–30.

Montgomery, Helen Barrett. *Centenary Translation of the New Testament.* Philadelphia: American Baptist, 1924.

One of the few translations of the Bible by a woman, this effort by a Baptist educator and denominational executive is preferred by many because of its sensitivity to unnecessarily sexist language. It is kept in print by Judson Press as *The New Testament in Modern English.*

Pape, Dorothy R. *In Search of God's Ideal Woman.* Downers Grove, Ill.: Inter-Varsity, 1976.

A missionary's somewhat personal interaction with the New Testament texts on women.

Penn-Lewis, Jessie. *The "Magna Carta" of Woman Accord-*

ing to the Scriptures. Bournemouth, Eng.: The Over-
comer Book Room, 1919.
Actually a summary of Katherine Bushnell's much
longer book God's Word to Women, this book has
been reprinted by Bethany Fellowship (1975).

Prohl, Russell C. Woman in the Church: A Restudy of
Woman's Place in Building the Kingdom. Grand Rapids: Eerdmans, 1957.
An important defense of the ministry of women by
a pastor in the Lutheran Church–Missouri Synod.

Roberts, Benjamin Titus. Ordaining Women. Rochester:
Earnest Christian, 1891.
This is the most radically egalitarian of the various
nineteenth-century evangelical defenses of feminism
and the ordination of women. Roberts, founder of the
Free Methodist Church, argues primarily on Biblical
grounds. This book has been reprinted in a modern
edition, with an introduction by Donald W. Dayton,
by Light and Life Press (1976).

Ruether, Rosemary Radford, ed. Religion and Sexism. New
York: Simon and Schuster, 1974.
A collection of essays describing the "images of wom-
en" in Jewish and Christian traditions from Biblical
times to the present. Largely the work of women feminist scholars in mainstream and liberal traditions.

Ryrie, Charles C. The Place of Women in the Church. New
York: Macmillan, 1958.
This conservative treatment of the question affirms
the role of women to be "subordination and honor in
the home, silence and helpfulness in the church" (p.
146). This book has been reprinted by Moody Press
as The Role of Women in the Church.

Scanzoni, Letha, and Hardesty, Nancy. All We're Meant
to Be. Waco, Tex: Word, 1974.
Selected as "book of the year" by Eternity magazine,
this has been the most influential of recent evangelical books advocating feminism. Written on the popular
level, it treats the whole range of issues (from Biblical
through family life to singleness). A paperback edition contains a study guide.

Scanzoni, Letha. "The Feminists and the Bible." Christianity
Today, 2 February 1973, pp. 10–15.
An historical study that shows the extent to which the

early feminists of the last century were working sincerely with the Scriptures.

Scroggs, Robin. "Paul and the Eschatological Woman." *Journal of the American Academy of Religion* 40 (1972): 283–303.

This much-discussed article argues that Paul was the "only certain spokesman for the liberation and equality of women in the New Testament"—but achieves this goal by insisting that the difficult passages are non-Pauline glosses or interpolations.

Smith, Charles Ryder. *The Bible Doctrine of Womanhood in Its Historical Evolution.* London: Epworth, 1923.

This older study from British Methodism argues for the equality of women on the basis that in the Scriptures there is a progressive movement in that direction.

Stanton, Elizabeth Cady, ed. *The Woman's Bible.* 2 vols. New York: European, 1898.

Probably the most famous of the feminist treatments of Scripture, this represents the more radical anticlerical wing of feminism. Its character is perhaps better indicated by the title given a modern reprint, *The Original Feminist Attack on the Bible* (New York: Arno, 1974). A modern paperback edition is also available from the Coalition Task Force on Women and Religion, 4759 15th Ave. NE, Seattle, WA 98105.

Starr, Lee Anna. *The Bible Status of Women.* New York: Revell, 1926.

Lee Anna Starr, a pastor in the Methodist Protestant Church, argues for an egalitarian reading of the Scripture on the basis of close study in the original languages. An appendix includes an essay by German church historian Harnack, arguing that Priscilla was the author of the Epistle to the Hebrews. Originally published by one of the largest evangelical publishers, this 416-page treatise is now kept in print by the Pillar of Fire (Zarephath, New Jersey), a small denomination founded by Alma White, an ardent feminist who greatly admired Starr and her book.

Stendahl, Krister. *The Bible and the Role of Women.* Translated by Emilie T. Sander. Philadelphia: Fortress, 1966.

This short but already-classic study by a Harvard Divinity School New Testament scholar was originally prompted by the debates on the ordination of women in the Lutheran State Church of Sweden. Stendahl treats the problem as one of "hermeneutics," or the question of precisely how the Biblical material is to function as authority for life today in a culture vastly different from that of the New Testament.

Swidler, Leonard. "Jesus Was a Feminist." *Catholic World* 212 (1970–71): 177–83.

A famous article arguing that, viewed against the Jewish background of His age, Jesus' treatment of women was so revolutionary that it can only be called feminist.

Tavard, George H. *Woman in Christian Tradition.* Notre Dame: University of Notre Dame, 1973.

An important study in the Catholic tradition, this book is a Biblical, historical, and theological treatment of the question. Consideration is also given to Protestant and Eastern Orthodox positions.

Thrall, Margaret E. *The Ordination of Women to the Priesthood.* London: SCM, 1958.

This defense of the ordination of women is rooted in an analysis of the early chapters of Genesis that pits the first chapter (egalitarian) against the second (subordinationist).

Trible, Phyllis. "Depatriarchalizing in Biblical Interpretation." *Journal of the American Academy of Religion* 41 (1973): 30–48.

An Old Testament professor at Andover-Newton Theological School here finds already within the Old Testament instances of the overcoming of patriarchal structures and movement toward the equality of women. Abridged as "The Bible and Women's Liberation," *Theology Digest* 22 (1974): 32–37.

Vos, Clarence J. *Woman in Old Testament Worship.* Delft: Judels and Brinkman, 1968.

A careful study of the role of women in the Old Testament as this sheds light on the modern question of the ordination of women.

Zerbst, Fritz. *The Office of Woman in the Church.* St. Louis: Concordia, 1955.

Considered by some to be the best book-length argument against the ordination of women.

DONALD W. DAYTON
Director of Mellander Library
Assistant Professor of Theology
North Park Theological Seminary

# Index of Authors

# Index of Scripture